Everyday People Everyday Leaders

Lessons in leadership
from the stories of everyday people

COLIN TAPSCOTT

ISBN:9798651139163

For my family,
my pack, my strength

CONTENTS

Preface

Leadership: a word traditionally reserved for those with a title, a badge, a position, a name, an office, a desk, some stripes on the arm or a story of heroism to tell. But in my experience, starting as the son of a farmhand, leadership is simpler and more pervasive than that.

> Howard Gardner believes that leadership 'is the ability to tell a story that affects the thoughts, feelings and actions of others'. [i]
>
> Seth Godin believes that leadership is 'the ability to believe in something, tell the story of change, to go there and others follow'. [ii]

I believe that leadership can be found in the poorest and quietest of places, away from the media and award ceremonies. It can be found in everyday places, exhibited by everyday people being everyday leaders.

This book tells the story of a few of these everyday leaders that I have met and a couple more famous ones that I have not met. Each story demonstrates an aspect of how to lead effectively, so that when you piece them together you complete the jigsaw of leadership. The good news for those wanting to be a leader is that you don't have to have all the pieces of the jigsaw to start. Like the childhood football sticker albums, it is the journey of gathering the precious stickers that is part of the enjoyment. Central to the principle of being a good leader is being flexible, willing to learn and develop as a leader and gathering new skills as you practise the art of leadership. Read on and hopefully discover that you have some skills already and you can, as with the sticker album, collect others as you journey through leadership.

Chapter 1: Redefine failure

Matt, Jenny and Colin

"It is important for us to start with reality. Leadership is hard. Leadership does not always go smoothly. Leadership will have downs as well as ups. Leadership will have dark nights of the soul, sleepless nights and feelings of inadequacy. If we don't start with this reality of leadership, we set our leaders up for seeing failure as their fault, as opposed to part of their leadership journey where moments of failure are learning points. The leader has enough to contend with, without doing battle with the dementors of self-doubt and loneliness."

Moving on

He slowly pulled the door closed, the echo of the latch seeming to ring in his ears. He looked one last time through the inspection window as he reluctantly turned the lock. It had been ten years, almost to the day, since he opened the same door for the first time and stepped into leading this large school through the challenge of improvement. Ten years of hard work, ten years of vision casting, ten years of problem solving. And now, it was over. Time for the next challenge.

If this were a movie, there would now be a flashback sequence. It would start with a scene of working on the farm as a teenager, loading bales on the trailer. A scene of hard work, sweat, grit and determination. It would move on to study in the lecture room, closely followed by the first job in teaching, highlighting the thrill of enlightening students and seeing them learn. It would move to working in schools making a difference to children from poor communities, mixing the joy of laughter, the strength of relationships to help them learn. And then it would freeze frame at the first morning of the job of amalgamating two schools at his first headship. The sense of bewilderment as to how he had got that huge first headship at 30, mixed with the raw passion for making it a success. And then it would fast forward to first stepping through that same door that he had just locked. Walking through the door of a school that had lost its way, in a community where many didn't realise that their children had amazing potential. The movie would later have the hero walking off with personal belongings to fight another day, fuelled by the success of his last venture.

But this is not the movies. This is reality. And what the movie failed to show is the reason the door was being locked on that Sunday afternoon in March, the reason there was no-one there apart from his wife. The reason was that this is the reality of leadership. Leadership has its lows as well as its highs and this is where the mettle of leadership is refined and strengthened. Only one hour earlier he had received a phone call from the CEO of the Academy chain he had worked for to say that following the Ofsted the previous week where there was missing reference paperwork. If he was to enter the building on Monday he would be suspended and escorted from the building, but if he were to resign with immediate effect then this could be avoided. Despite him giving the Academy chain 10 months' notice that he would be leaving in September anyway, their timeframe was somewhat shorter. Some would see the missing paperwork as a shared responsibility of the headteacher, governors, Academy chain and those whose department it was in. He was quite prepared, as headteacher, to take responsibility to repair the problem. That's what leaders do. But this was not to be the ending in this story.

Some might say that this is not the best way to start a book on leadership. Leadership is about success over challenge and how when you do the right thing the hero leader gets the right result. Of course, this book, like many books on leadership, will try to give you stories, examples, key phrases, top tips and strategy on how to lead well. But I think it is also important for us to start with reality. Leadership is hard. Leadership does not always go smoothly. Leadership will have downs as well as ups. Leadership will have dark nights of the soul, sleepless nights and feelings of inadequacy. If we don't start with this reality of leadership, we set our leaders up for seeing failure as their fault, as opposed to part of their leadership journey where moments of failure are learning points. The leader has enough to contend with in dealing with the problem at hand, without doing battle with the dementors of self-doubt and loneliness.

You see, although it happens to all leaders, failure rarely gets a mention in the movies or the books. Yet, over time, it contributes to the measure of leaders' success when they seek to understand it, plan and grow from it.

A great leader

If you go to the National Portrait gallery, you can see a picture of Sir Winston Churchill painted by Sir William Orpen in 1916. This was painted way before his historic "We'll fight them on the beaches" speech and leadership. Viewing it for the first time, I saw a younger, slimmer Churchill than the usual pictures of this famous leader. What struck me though, was his eyes. They were troubled, haunted. I stood there for ages, watching them, sensing a sadness of the soul and a synchronicity. And then I read the descriptor next to it.

Statesman. As First Lord of the Admiralty during World War 1, Churchill was held responsible for the naval campaign to capture the Dardanelles Straits from the Ottoman Empire that resulted in 46,000 allied deaths. He resigned in 1915, his reputation ruined until the Dardanelles Commission cleared his name in 1917. Orpen's portrait was painted during the Dardanelles enquiry and captures Churchill at the lowest point of his career. Orpen referred to him as a 'man of misery' at that time. Churchill remarked: 'It is not the picture of a man, it is a picture of a man's soul'.

If Churchill can come back from that situation of public blame to lead his country in the second world war as Prime Minister, then any of us can come back from our perceived 'failures' too. This book, and many others, can share principles of leadership that help success, but we must understand that leadership will have the sine curve of success and failure. Failure, on its own, is not what causes the damage. It is the lack of learning from it that causes the long-term impact.

Kintsugi approach

Matthew Syed, in his book Black Box Thinking[iii], explains that the single greatest obstacle to progress is failing to learn from mistakes, and discusses how we need to redefine failure in order to unleash progress, creativity and resilience. Redefining failure as part of a learning process is crucial for a leader. I want to build on Matthew Syed's principle and add that we need to have a 'Kintsugi' approach in our leadership.

Kintsugi is the Japanese art of repairing broken pottery with lacquer dusted or mixed with powdered gold, silver or platinum. As a philosophy, it treats breakage and repair as part of the history of an object, rather than something to disguise. 'Kintsugi' leadership tells the story of battles lost and learnt from, that fuel the battles that are then won. It tells a story of a leader far greater than first thought, as they were flexible enough to learn from the things that didn't work, brave enough to travel from defeat to victory in order to help find success in the things that then can work. For example, Churchill's story of WW2 victory is far greater with the knowledge of the Kintsugi scars of the Dardanelles Straits.

For anyone who has found themselves in the midst of failure, they will know that redefining failure as a learning process is challenging. Emotions are high, but the secret is to develop your mindset.

Leadership mindsets

I have been privileged to work with the organisation Emerging Leaders in the last 3 years. This charity works with vulnerable communities in the world, enabling them to face extreme challenges with their Leadership for Life programme[iv]. This programme has at its core the principle that everybody has the ability to lead at some level in their lives.

Our performance is inhibited by interference: poor thinking mindsets that try to pull us down. Our mindsets aren't fixed and we can reset them from an old way of thinking to unlock our potential through the discipline of practising new leadership mindsets. Foundational to this is that if you 'change your thinking, you can change your life'. Emerging Leaders suggests 7 key leadership mindsets that can replace the poor thinking to help us lead ourselves. These are:

1. Lift up your head
2. See yourself as a leader
3. See and take responsibility
4. Be proactive
5. Change something
6. Focus
7. Appreciative thinking

When the failure, error or mistakes happen, a leader needs to employ these leadership mindsets. **Lifting up their head** from the frustration, sadness, anger and getting a perspective on how big it actually is and who and what is around to help. **Seeing themselves as a leader**, they **see and take responsibility** for the action and **change something** to make it better.

There are countless stories of this leadership mindset process in famous inventors. James Dyson had 5,127 attempts before making his cyclone vacuum cleaner. JK Rowling had 12 publishers reject her Harry Potter novels before Bloomsbury took them on. Thomas Edison is famously meant to have quoted about his approach to inventing the light bulb, "I have not failed. I've just found 10,000 ways that won't work."

Being a 'redefining leader' is not just the privilege of the famous. There are also the everyday stories of everyday people redefining failure as a learning point, as a challenge to be overcome.

Redefining Leaders

Jenny – overcoming every challenge

Jenny sat there. A tear trickled down her cheek. "Jenny, I am delighted to offer you the post of class teacher," were the words faintly reverberating around her head.

"I'm sorry," she said, wiping the tear from her eye. "I just can't believe that I've finally done it."

This wasn't just any old success story of someone getting their first teaching job. These were tears of sweat, hard work, determination and pain. And I had seen her go through most of it.

In 1997, Jenny had left school with 1 GCSE following a period of illness in her final two years of schooling. She left school and took up working in a pub. That 1 GCSE did not credit Jenny with the challenge she had faced and certainly could not reward her with her heart's desire of training to be a teacher. For many, that setback would break them and potentially define the course of their subsequent life. But not Jenny.

After completing a nursery nurse diploma, in Jan 2000 she got a job working as a teaching assistant in a school. She was like a sponge, willing to learn at every opportunity how best to work with children. Alongside her Teaching Assistant job, she worked in a pub, whilst she studied on a 'Specialist Teaching Assistant' course, gaining credits for the next stage of her journey. In 2005 she enrolled on her three-year journey to gain her degree, first by completing a two-year Foundation degree in Early Years, then a third year to gain her Honours degree in Early Learning.

In 2008 she passed and started her new challenge of gaining the all-important English and Maths GSCEs. She attended college three nights a week and was thrilled to achieve recognised grades. At last could apply for teacher training. Her references from the school were glowing. She took part in the assessment day and finally the envelope landed on the doormat with the result of her application. "No, you have not passed selection".

The blow was crushing, but all those who worked around Jenny knew that she would make a great teacher. Deep down, Jenny knew that too. Twelve months later, she applied again. She had worked hard on areas that had previously held her back. She attended selection day, nervous but determined. Envelope day arrived again. Slowly, hesitantly, she opened the envelope. There, in bold letters. "I am sorry to tell you that you have been unsuccessful."

Now Jenny is a hero in my eyes, but she is human. She did cry. It did hurt. But one of the characteristics of a leader is knowing when to seek help when you are determined to achieve. I had seen Jenny's journey, her growth, her determination. And so, when a new 'Assessment Only' route was established, I put her forward. I received the phone call from the training college with the verdict. I sat Jenny down, and said the words she had been longing to hear. "Jenny, you have been accepted to train as a teacher." Tears trickled down her face then and nine months later, she sat in that same chair and the tears began again as she heard those words that were now faintly reverberating around her head. "Jenny, I am delighted to offer you the post of class teacher." Every challenge she had met had hurt. However, she had accepted, analysed to see what she could improve, worked at it and, like Edison, Dyson & Rowling, seen it as a challenge to overcome. Jenny has humility abounding, a lovely caring nature, and is, without doubt, one of the best 'leaders of yourself' I have worked with.

Matt's A Levels

It was summer 2015. As a family, we were in the south of France on holiday. But it was AS Level results time and my son Matt was awaiting his results via email. Internet signal was a bit ropey after a huge electrical storm the night before, but finally through tethering to my phone the email had downloaded. Expectantly, Matt opened the email to see how he had done. The look of expectation suddenly drained from him and he went quiet. He had studied hard; I had seen him revising. But the email declared he had only passed one out of four and even that one was nowhere near what he had expected.

He went quiet and we knew he needed space. We told him we loved him, were proud of who he was and would support him in any decision he wanted to now take. But we were hurting for him. We needn't have worried about him though, as his response was one of a leader. A leader of himself. He took some time to be quiet, to give himself a pep talk. He took time to talk to us and reflect on his options. And on our return from holiday, he asked for a meeting with his Head of sixth form to discuss his options and request to restart his A levels again. He picked four different A levels, perhaps better suited to his aptitudes and interests. One year later he had four good AS grades and, after another year, he gained high A Level grades (ABC). He lifted up his head, saw those around who could help him. He saw himself as a leader of his life, took responsibility for the situation, changed what he did to better suit him and then focused on his work for the next two years. He did not let failure define him as a victim. He let failure define him as a leader.

Taking the team with you

I've always felt that communication was one of my strengths. I get on well with people and develop good relationships.

Working with my senior team in each school I have worked in has always been a key part of how I have led. But on one occasion in my last school, I nearly lost my senior team's trust because I didn't consider the impact of a decision.

My senior team was great. They were hard working, passionate about serving the needs of the children in our community, and we had a good balance where they were supportive of me and the vision but were able to professionally challenge and discuss things. However, I had identified that there was an increasing workload at the top of the organisation; my deputy head, Lisa, and I were not keeping on top of paperwork, strategy and supporting colleagues to develop.

We identified that we could do with another person at senior level and so we spoke to governors about the need for restructuring and how duties could be distributed. They supported this suggestion and we spoke to the wider senior team about it. At this point, all seemed ok. We arranged interviews and two candidates came out as having superb credentials: one internal candidate, Gemma, an emotionally intelligent, hard-working member of the team, and a second, Lauren, an external candidate with exceptional drive and understanding of learning for children. It was a complete tie for different strengths but we could not split them. It was one of those moments where we knew we needed both. A few phone calls and review of the budget and we took the plunge.

The decision was excellent for what they brought to the team and the school. Head, deputy and two assistant heads – the 'headship team', as we became known – worked brilliantly together and we saw instant impact on workload and support and development of staff. But inadvertently I had created a problem with my wider senior leadership. We still met as a team, we still discussed strategy and problem solving together. But in reality, by creating the 'headship team' of four, I had brought in a layer of leadership that the former senior leaders had not had above them.

Sometimes the headship team had discussed issues before coming to the senior team. It therefore created a sense for some of what I call 'Blue Peter leadership'. Just like the craft making on the kids' TV programme, where presenters would say, "Here is one I made earlier," we produced the leadership version of "Here's a decision I made earlier."

This was one of those decisions where I had not foreseen the consequences of what on the surface was a really good decision. I then had to take time and energy to rebuild some trust with the team. I arranged some group coaching to help us examine the best way to work together going forward and as a team we had to concentrate and be purposeful in decision making together. We got there because they were a good team and we worked hard on it. In my current role, advising leaders on change management, I advise much more communication, discussion and clarity and consideration of consequences than I used on that occasion, to hopefully avoid the inadvertent feelings of devaluation that I created.

7 practical steps to redefine failure

The stories sound great, perhaps inspiring even, as you might expect from a leadership book. But how do you practically lift yourself from a failure and use it as a learning point? Failures can be big or small. Whether it is being exited from a job or just meetings that don't go so well; targets not met or a set of results that are not so good. Whatever size they are, here are some steps that you can take when you are facing failure and you need to redefine it.

1. Give yourself a bit of time

Let's be honest, when things go wrong you are not likely to be feeling top form. Your emotions can be raw and the cognitive, creative thinking part of your brain is probably suffering from a bit of a cortisol stress flood, so you won't be the most inventive. Cortisol is the stress hormone that the body releases that chronically affects the brain cells in the hippocampus, the area of the brain involved with memory, learning, and emotional regulation. When we are chronically stressed the electrical signals in the brain associated with memories weaken, whilst the areas in the brain associated with emotions strengthen.

Rest is one of several things that help reduce cortisol. So taking some time to process and step back allows the cortisol to reduce so that the cognitive part of your brain can start to engage again. If you can, write down exactly what happened as near to the event as you can. The memory can forget and substitute things in time. The reflection can then happen the next day onwards, when your emotions have settled. If you are in a high stress situation that demands immediate attention, it might feel like you do not have time. Even in these situations, just grabbing five minutes to walk around and gather your thoughts can help you make a better decision.

2. Get perspective

When 'failure' first happens, it feels all-consuming. Sometimes it can feel like our world is caving in, like the sky in the children's story of *Chicken Licken*. But, in most cases, it is not actually falling in. So, unlike Chicken Licken, take time to review your situation. Consider whether the sky has actually fallen in or whether it is one small problem amidst a range of other more positive things.

When it first became clear that the inspection team had found some paperwork issues in March 2017, it felt as if the blood was draining from my body. All of the positive comments about teaching and learning from the lead inspector before that moment became insignificant; I sensed all of the hard work was to no avail as we were facing a bad judgement due to missing references. But as I sat down that night, I asked myself, "Has anyone died?" I felt like I was going to have a heart attack that day, but I was still alive. "What is the rest of my life like? Do I have friends and family that love me? If I lose my job, is there life beyond it?" Now, the fact I am writing this book, have established a leadership development company that gets great reviews and I am in fact happier in my work than I have been for years, indicates that this 'failure' was not the end. In fact I learnt a lot about people, about what really matters in life and I spent the first three months telling every headteacher that I met to "go and personally check your paperwork". You'll never guess... They too found errors. Fortunately, sharing with them my situation saved them from the same fate as me.

3. Get support

If you are struggling to get perspective, then getting the right people around you is key to reviewing what happened and how to improve it the next time. The right people are those a) you trust; b) who can tell it to you straight; c) who are emotionally intelligent and know when it is the right time to chat about it.

In 2010, one of our most loved teachers in my school, Toni Andrews, died following a battle with bowel cancer. I had been told late one evening that this had happened and the following morning I knew I needed to tell staff that day. I had planned to tell them at the end of the day, so as not to consume them with grief and sadness all day, but wisely chose to consult my Senior Leadership Team.

They advised to bring staff together before school and tell them, and to tell children and parents at the end of the day. I knew it was the right decision as they stood with me on it. It proved to be the case, as staff appreciated being told and to have the time together during the day to remember her. Being a leader does not mean that you have to face things alone. You don't need to have all the answers, just the wisdom to know how to find them.

4. Review – say what you see/what happened

Reviewing what happened, in order to find a better way next time, needs to be open and honest. Reviewing starts by saying what you see. Look at a) how you dealt with it; b) how others dealt with it; c) what impact the environment had on the situation and d) anything about the incident itself. State it factually.

5. Analyse – WWW, EBI

Then ask yourself first, what worked well (WWW). In any situation there will normally be good things. These are the things that don't need to change. Then ask what would be 'even better if' (EBI) you did it differently?

6. Identify the key thing that needs to change

Once you have your analysis from step 5, consider which one thing needs to be changed that would potentially have the biggest impact. Look for the thing that would make the most difference, ideally with the least effort.

7. Work with others to have this as the focus

This 'one thing' is now your focus. Preach it to the masses, make sure that everyone knows about the new focus. Run with it and then ask again, "Has it worked?"

Failure – just preparing you for the next step

Imagine if, as a baby, after that first attempt to walk, we plonked down on our padded bottom and said, "That's it, I've failed to walk. I'm not trying that again." Wouldn't life be funny with all these grown-ups in pushchairs! But then who would be pushing the pushchairs, if we had all given up on walking, because we failed that first time?

At some point, we can hit that sense of hopelessness. Hopelessness that feels like you're trapped at the bottom of a dark pit with impossibly high walls all around you. It is leadership that gets you out of that pit. Leadership is not as complicated as some might have you believe. Leadership can be found in everyday people in everyday places. Leadership can be found in the toughest situations. It is leaders telling their own story that in turn affects the thoughts, feelings and actions of others. Leadership is what helps you climb the impossibly high walls of frustration, disappointment and hopelessness. If the son of a farmhand, like me, can lead himself through the challenge of that day in March 2017, then anyone can. Let me introduce you in the following pages to people I have met, all of whom demonstrate the characteristics needed of a good leader.

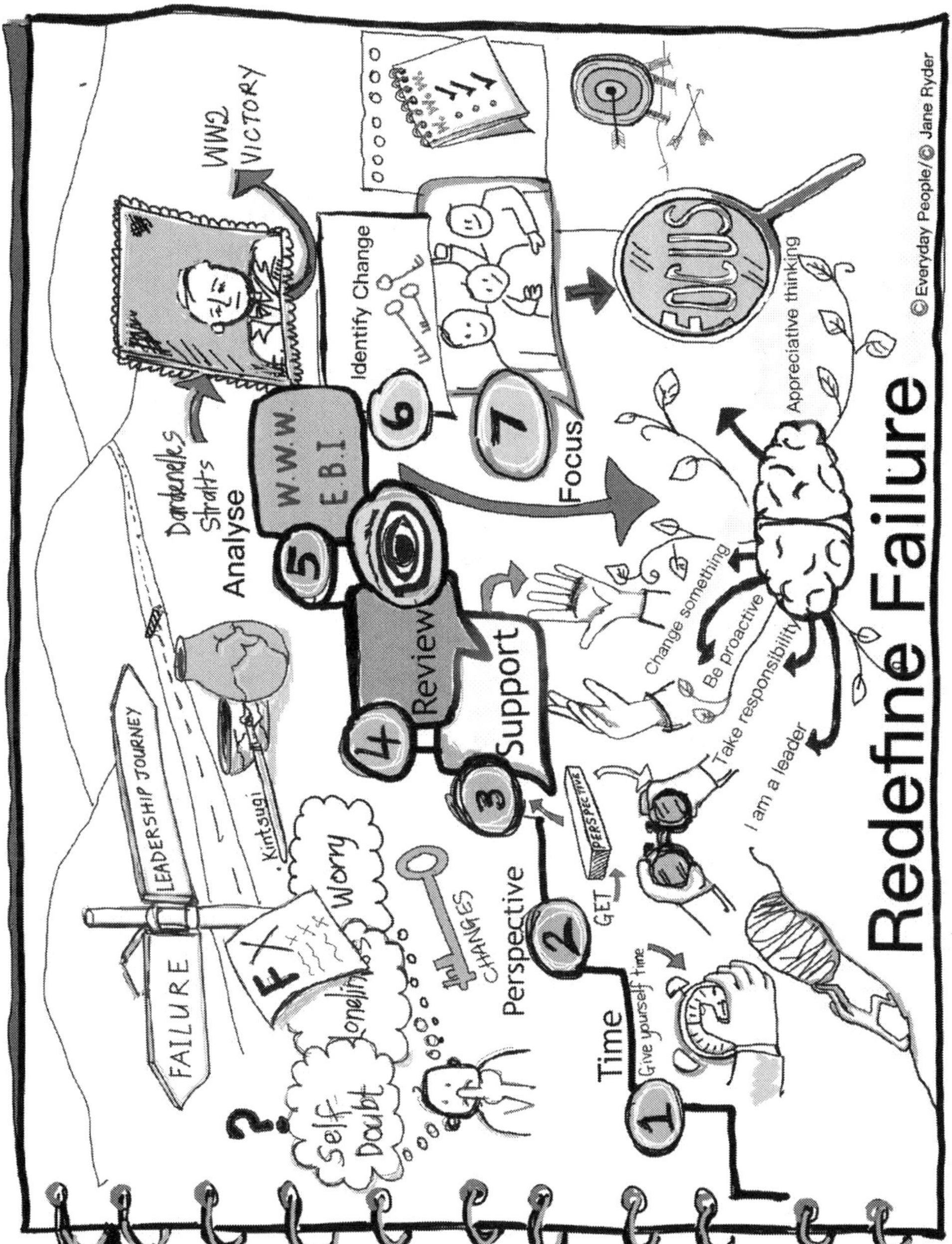
Redefine Failure
FAILURE
LEADERSHIP JOURNEY
Kintsugi
Self Doubt
Loneliness
Worry
CHANGES
Time
Give yourself time
Perspective
GET
PERSPECTIVE
Support
Review
Analyse
W.W.W.
E.B.I.
Dardanelles Straits
WW2 VICTORY
Identify Change
Focus
FOCUS
I am a leader
Take responsibility
Be proactive
Change something
Appreciative thinking
© Everyday People/© Jane Ryder

Personal Reflection – Redefine Failure

Failure
1. Where have I 'failed'?
2. What thoughts do I have about that 'failure?
3. In what ways is that helpful/unhelpful?
4. What did I learn from it?

A RAG review is reviewing how you perform using a simple traffic light colour system of Red, Amber and Green.

Red – Not performing well
Amber – performance is mixed
Green – a good, strong performance

On the next page you will be asked to use this approach to reflect on your use of the 7 steps.

Personal Reflection – Redefine Failure

7 Practical Steps		
If something goes wrong, how do I use these 7 steps? RAG (Red, Amber, Green) how you use them.		
Practical Step	RAG	How I can develop
Give yourself a bit of time		
Get perspective		
Get support		
Review – say what you see/what happened		
Analyse – WWW, EBI		
Identify key thing that needs to change (to have best impact)		
Work with others to have this as the focus		

Next Steps	
What works well for me? (WWW)	What could be 'even better if' I changed? (EBI)

Chapter 2: Inspire

Dave, Hannah and Trevor

"Inspiring is about resonating something in the soul of another... You cannot keep breathing life into others if you are not refuelling and replenishing yourself. For you to keep telling the story with inspiration, passion, purpose and being heartfelt, you have to refresh yourself."

The power of story

Just spend 5 minutes with Dave Hannah and I guarantee that you will be enthralled by his thinking. Dave talks passionately about the importance of young people, the importance of a safe haven for young people, the importance of good role models for young people, the importance of providing quality relationship-based youth counselling and the importance of volunteers and community. But what embeds this vision is when he talks about the poor relationship he has with his own dad and the importance of the male role models who showed him a better way when he was growing up.

Dave ran an amazing youth provision called The Mix, in Stowmarket in Suffolk. Now, the building is impressive and cool and many locals think it is a nightclub rather than a youth provision. But it is not just about the building. It is about the intrinsic value of young people that resonates from Dave through every staff member.

The Mix was founded on building quality relationships with the young people that it serves. It was structured to generate its own income and it aimed to be able to sustain its core services through their own commercial activities within two years. So when you speak to the bookings manager they know their role is not just to book rooms, but they are an income generator that helps to provide a safe haven for young people. When you speak to the catering manager they know that their role is to cook great food for the young people and to generate income to support the work.
The ultimate testament to this vision for youth is that 80% of staff team is under 24. The story is alive.

Now, I am sure there are days when things are tough and hard and the young people they work with struggle to show their appreciation. But what keeps them going is the story that Dave told them; about creating a place for the Daves of today where they can discover their intrinsic worth and the person that they could be.

It's the story that they are helping to tell. And this storytelling all starts from Dave passionately inspiring others. Howard Gardner said that 'leadership is the ability to tell a story that affects the thoughts, feelings and actions of others.' [v] The key here, is to find connection from the story-teller to the listener. Dave has learnt to tell a story of hope for young people, a hope that connects and resonates with the others in his organisation. Seth Godin, in his book Tribes, said, "People don't believe what you tell them. They rarely believe what you show them. They often believe what their friends tell them. They always believe what they tell themselves."[vi] So, inspiring people is actually the ability to tell a story that intrinsically connects with their story, the story that they want to tell.

Key components

Inspiring people, like all leadership skills, does not happen by accident. Inspiring has 5 key components:

- Have a manifesto to connect
- Tell a story of the future that resonates
- Tell the story from the heart
- Model it
- Refresh yourself to keep telling the story – 'in-spire' to inspire

Manifesto to connect

The word manifesto perhaps now has a bad press, being seen as a political word where a political party puts forward the policies that they want you to vote them in on. A manifesto that, for many, rarely comes to fruition and feels like it was a book of broken promises.

But try not to see a manifesto in these terms. Manifesto simply means 'published verbal declaration of the intentions, motives, or views of the issuer'.

But a good manifesto tells the story of a future hope. Blake Mycoskie, when he set up TOMS (Tomorrow's Shoes) as a student, told others of the hope he had to help children who had no shoes. It was a belief that things didn't have to stay as they were. It was a narrative of how the future could tell a better story than the present. It was a story that connected with the basic human instinct that it is not fair for children to be treated this way and resonates with our human nature to want to nurture and care for the vulnerable. Dave Hannah's story at The Mix of bringing hope to young people resonates because his story is one where he is the living embodiment of the story he now wants to tell. It resonates with those who have had good role models or parenting because they want it for others. It resonates with those who have not had it because they don't want anyone else to experience the life that they had.

"Let me show you this." Andy, an inspirational designer friend of mine, handed me a small book. Glossy cover, cool photo on the cover. As I turned the pages, I recognised the picture on the inside of a mutual contact of ours who was a professional videographer. "It's his *Vade Mecum,*" chirped Andy. "I've been helping him develop it."

Now I have an O' level in Latin (long story and yes, I am that old), but I couldn't translate. Fortunately, Andy explained: "I've been helping him clarify exactly what it is he stands for and represents to clients and so I have worked with him to produce a *Vade Mecum."*

If you love a bit of Latin, it comes from *vāde* ("Go! Walk!") + *mēcum* ("with me"), literally meaning "go with me". A *Vade Mecum* used to be carried by ancient travellers as a handbook. It was like a traveller's guide, a kind of mixture of reference guide and testimony as to who they were and what they stood for. As a leader, it is crucial that we are clear on our purpose. It's crucial that we live and breathe our *Vade Mecum* or manifesto.

Leadership starts with leading ourselves, gaining clarity on our purpose and values. Once we have this, we are ready to lead others. We then repeat that pattern. When leading others it is crucial we are clear on the purpose of the organisation and where we are going and bring clarity in a way that will inspire.

A story of the future that resonates

Inspiring is about resonating something in the soul of another. Think of times that you have been inspired into action. Maybe it was an advert for a charity that stirred you to give. Maybe it was someone encouraging you to join them in an activity. What happens is that the words create a picture or story that resonates with a shared purpose or desire. Take, for example, the charity that invites you to 'come and join our group that rescues animals'. This might resonate with your need to be loved, to be part of a group. In particular, it resonates with your shared desire or purpose to help vulnerable animals. Once you then attend, see what they do in action, their radio wave of purpose synchronises with yours and you make music together.

Tell the story from the heart

Create 'meerkat moments'

My wife and I run a charity for children. It has no paid staff; everyone involved is a volunteer. This has been running since 2005 and in 2015 we invited volunteers to a meeting to consider our future and what events we should run. As volunteers sat before me that day we were at a junction point for the charity. We had run it for 10 years, with success, but we were unsure of the next steps to take. So I told them stories. Stories of Danny, the boy who had never been on holiday, until we took him on one of our charity holidays. Stories of Tom, the boy who came as a young lad and now was a young holiday leader. Each story a reminder of the core values the charity stood for.

What made each story so powerful is that they came from the heart, with honesty and integrity. These powerful personal stories resonate with the listener and spur them to continue helping others. What accompanied each one of these stories was me publicly thanking individuals for caring for the young people. This created what I call 'meerkat moments'. Like a meerkat that hears something and stands up, ears pricked, and looks around, publicly praising people causes us to listen, recognise the person who praises and encourages us to seek that same praise by copying the behaviour. Each time we meet, I constantly tell the stories that help people to understand what the vision for young people is, and in a way that helps the listener to see it as achievable for them too.

Standing on the tank

The staff I worked with in my last school were tremendous. Every day there were challenges and staff worked tirelessly for the children. I remember one occasion though, when there was a growing sense of unrest, due to the challenges that we faced. I had tried to chat through issues with a number of people but there still seemed to be an undercurrent of discontent. I sensed it was time to 'stand on the tank and rally the troops'. You may remember the war films, the scene when times are tough but the general calls his troops together and stands on a tank to be seen and heard. He reminds the troops of the purpose and the need for bravery and to fight as one. So I called the staff together. I reminded them that I was the son of a farmhand, that I came from a low-income family and that I wanted the children in our school to have the opportunity that I have had and that many of them have had too. I reminded them that we were going to do our best for these children, that it required hard work and commitment and that I needed every single person working together to achieve it. I recognised that these were hard times and would require immense effort and I could only go forward with those who could give it. I did not want to lose anyone, but if they felt they wanted to leave then I would do all I could to help them find a place that was right for them and we would do so together with maturity and friendship. It was heartfelt and honest and a tough message. As I stopped you could have heard a pin drop.

The vast majority came with me that day. There were a couple who then had honest chats with me about working together to find a better place for them, which I supported them with and they were happier in their new setting. The undercurrent dissipated immediately because the message was delivered with integrity.

Model it

I remember Hannah coming into my office in the school I was headteacher at in Stevenage. In 2003 I had asked her to head up the Early Years department in the school. Hannah Isher was an amazing Early Years teacher and I knew she had the skills to transform the department. "I'm not a leader, I can't stand up front and tell everyone what to do, it's just not me," she declared. What I knew, and that she then discovered, is that she was one of the best examples of a 'shepherd leader' that I have ever worked with. A shepherd walks amongst the sheep and guides. You see, Hannah knew what good Early Years practice looked like. She lived it, modelled it and was brilliant in the art of 'Miranda moments'. 'Miranda moments' are from the TV programme Miranda, when the star of the show, Miranda Hart, stops, turns to the camera and then explains to the audience watching what she is thinking or makes a facial gesture that explains a little secret to the audience behind the camera. Hannah had the ability to show her staff what to do and take those little moments to explain why she wanted it that way. She lifted people up and made them feel capable of copying it too. She held open departmental meetings where she asked their thoughts and ideas and drew them together to shape practice. In 2006, the school was awarded the Early Years chartermark, celebrating all that she had worked with her team to achieve.

'In-spire' to inspire

Trevor Waldock is the CEO and founder of Emerging Leaders. This charity seeks to bring leadership mindset training to the poorest communities in the world. It goes beyond the principle of 'send them food'. It goes beyond the principle of teach them how to farm or fish.

It teaches them problem solving mindsets so that when their next setback comes they have the capacity to see a way forward to solve the problem. Trevor and the team's work is inspirational. I had the privilege to meet those in Dandora in Nairobi who had participated in the training and to see the difference they were making in their community.

On one occasion, in a converted barn in Suffolk in January 2015, I met with some of the leaders from the charity to understand what they were doing. They were an inspirational group, and I felt inadequate in their presence. I remember Trevor explaining a simple thing about being inspirational that week. As I remember what he said, it almost felt like one of those 'time standing still moments' where you receive something that is like a jigsaw piece filling a gap that helps the world make a little more sense. In my mind's eye I can see him. He leant forward, like a wise sage. Time stopped... and he said:

"Inspire means to 'in-spire'; to breathe in. In order to inspire others you must 'in-spire'. In order to put life or breath into others you must breathe in yourself."

I have since understood the truth of that. You cannot keep breathing life into others, if you are not refuelling and replenishing yourself. For you to keep telling the story with heartfelt inspiration, passion and purpose, you have to refresh yourself. You have to refresh your thinking by reading, by discussing thinking with others, by experiencing. You have to refresh your body with rest, with sleep, with exercise, with food. You have to refresh your spirit with relationships, with love, with laughter, with fun. You have to refresh your soul with times of spiritual reflection, with worship and admiration of the beauty of our world. Remember, 'in-spire' to inspire.

Inspire
Manifesto
Story from the heart
Future
Refresh yourself
Model it
My story
HOPE
THOUGHTS
My story
Others
Vāde Mecum
in-spire
BREATHE LIFE
TOMS
HOPE
the MIX
resonate
My Manifesto~
HERE NOW
MY PURPO
Inspire to inspire
1
2
3
4
5
©Everyday People © Jane Ryder

Personal Reflection – Inspire

Manifesto
Do you have a 'manifesto'? What do you believe passionately that you want to be a future change for people? What would be in your '*Vade Mecum*'?
Manifesto
What is the purpose that resonates with others?
Who is it for?

Personal Reflection – Inspire

Inspire to Inspire		
RAG (Red, Amber, Green) rate the things you are doing to inspire yourself and consider actions you could take to improve this.		
Inspire items	RAG	Action
Read books/articles on leadership		
Read books/articles on your field		
Listen to podcasts/watch video/TED talks		
Time to reflect on current practice		
Times of rest		
Network to discuss leadership/your field		
Latest research on leadership		
Latest research on your field		

Meerkat Moments & Modelling	
Name 5 ways you model what you require	Name 5 things that could create a 'meerkat moment'

Chapter 3: Build Relationships

Liz, Shaun and Anna

"Pan back over time and you can see that interaction isn't generated as a modern day 'click & collect', instantaneous, quick fix solution. It is like gold refined in a furnace. It is fashioned with investment of time, listening, supporting, encouraging, challenging and celebrating."

Deep affiliation

"She's in the building, she's in the building," were the words that were passed on like a relay baton down the corridors of the school. Like an echoed sound wave, the movement of people reflected back down the corridors towards the staff room where 'she' sat drinking a cup of coffee with the headteacher. Cleaner, teaching assistant, teacher and senior staff all joined together in the corridor to see her. It had been less than a year since 'she' had left the school and now she had popped back in on her way back from a meeting to catch up with the headteacher for a cuppa. You had to be there to hear and understand the tone of reverence as the word 'she' was spoken. It was used with a sense of awe, excitement, friendship and uttermost respect. Imagine a mixture of the queen and your best friend that you hadn't seen for a year and maybe that comes close to the tone of the word 'she'. So, who was 'she'?

Liz Green, former deputy head, had worked at the school for 8 years. Sitting at the staff room table, sipping her coffee, it was as if Liz had never left. But she had. She was now a headteacher herself. Liz took another sip of coffee and updated me on how things were going in her own school. Suddenly, the door was flung open and in bounded one of my brilliant support staff. She couldn't control herself and sped towards Liz. There was a deep warmth in the hug that she gave Liz, far in excess of the pleasantries of 'How are you?', 'How are the kids?' that was shared between them.

Daniel Goleman lists six leadership styles[vii], one of which is 'affiliative'. This style is a 'people first' style, high on value and low on control. Like all styles it has to be used carefully and in balance with other styles of leadership. At its very best, affiliative leadership starts with listening to those you are working with. It is about investing time in people, understanding how they tick, seeing them as a whole person, understanding that the person at work will still have home issues in their mind at work and valuing their contribution.

The leader who uses this the best then blends this with the 'authoritative' style, explaining why the person needs to come with you on the journey of improvement as an individual and as an organisation. If you wanted a human personification of this style, you would find it in Liz Green.

When you watch a good magician perform, it creates a sense of awe. However carefully you watch them, you can't work out how they do it. Watching Liz Green in action, I was often in awe. In awe of her ability to make connection with people, her ability to persuade someone to engage. It could be easy to think that this skill is just for the few. But watch people like Liz carefully and you can evaluate what she does to build relationships so naturally.

Take her relationship with the teaching assistant who embraced her with deep warmth in the staffroom. Pan back over time and you can see that type of hug wasn't generated as a modern day 'click & collect', instantaneous, quick fix solution. It was like gold refined in a furnace. It was fashioned with investment of time, listening, supporting, encouraging, challenging and celebrating. The teaching assistant was one of our best. She cared for children, especially the vulnerable, and built relationships with them. She was able to understand gaps in their learning and their emotional development and teach in simple ways to help them move on. But, in the early days, she had lacked confidence in who she was and how good she was. Liz had regularly sat next to her and shared a cuppa and had asked her about her family. She took time to praise the talent she saw in her, encouraging her to try new things and praised her when they had gone well. Liz had been willing to mentor her, giving her rich feedback with encouragement and challenge. In time, her confidence grew and that teaching assistant went on to support and mentor others in the way she had been mentored by Liz.

Trust-centred relationship

The ability as a leader to generate a deep warmth, trust and respect towards you from those in your team comes not from just being friendly and kind. Our primary role as a leader is not to generate friendships and to be liked. Our primary role is to lead. Leading well requires us to take people with us and to do this they need to respect you and your message of transition, change and improvement. We can get real shift in improvement when we have a clear purpose and alignment to that purpose. Relationships with one another, understanding each other's perspective, knowing our passions and interests helps us generate alignment as it enables deep trust to be built. Trusting a message alone is hard and it comes much easier when you have a relationship and deep trust in the person who is delivering it. At the core of a good relationship is trust. So how, as a leader, do you develop a trust-centred relationship

Work to build trust

Building on the work of Maister, Green & Galford in their book *The Trusted Advisor*, I think there are 5 areas in a work and leadership context that help trust to ARISE.

- Authenticity
- Reliability
- Intimacy
- Selflessness
- Expertise

Authenticity

People like authenticity. Imagine thinking your watch was a real Rolex and then discovering that it is a fake. There is huge disappointment. It is the same with people. We like to know what we are dealing with and what we see is what we get. We want to know that in a difficult time the person can be relied upon, that they are honest in all circumstances and that they will show integrity, even under pressure. Trust is like a bridge between two people and when we build a bridge we want to know that the footings that we have placed our bridge on are secure and have integrity. So, how consistent we are is crucial to this. How we talk about people in all circumstances, whether the person is present or not demonstrates our authenticity. I read a story recently of someone who applied for an internal promotion at work. The role required high levels of confidentiality and they did not get the role. They asked their boss afterwards why they did not get the role when they had never shared anything confidential from work. The boss acknowledged this, but politely pointed out some of the things he had shared in the office about other people, many of which were sensitive and private issues. If you take one thing from this book, it must be this:

Our character is who walks through the door
when no-one is looking.

Many great leaders have fallen when they forget this and allow their honesty to be eroded by quick wins or short cuts and then they are caught out later on. This phrase means that we consistently act well, even if we could get away with it. That demonstrates authenticity. Authenticity means that when the mistakes are made (because we are all human and can make mistakes), we own up to it and take responsibility.

Being authentic is also important when there are challenging moments. Sometimes, when listening to someone share the issue they are grappling with, I can sense an issue that they are not yet fully aware of. Being honest with people, even with hard truths, in a way that builds them up, helps them see that you are for them and therefore this generates trust. It is all about the way that you raise it. For example, if someone is being abrupt with their colleagues, then a phrase that might help could be: "Fred, you are a good friend that I want to support. I don't know if there are things troubling you at the moment, but I have noticed that you have been a bit abrupt in your tone to Betty and Barnie in the last two days. Is there anything I can help you with?"

Reliability

People want to know that the leader is consistent. Consistency brings security as they know what to expect of their leader. Having high expectations of yourself and others is a key part of this. Whenever you promise something and deliver on it, it reassures followers of your consistency and that you can be relied upon. The biggest developer of trust comes when you take responsibility for your actions and the situation. Take, for example, a particularly challenging parent in the school community. "I'm not happy. I'm going to the press," he said as he met me in the school foyer. He then explained how a member of staff had not dealt with his child correctly. I'd overheard the incident and, on this rare occasion, the member of staff had indeed not got it right. On most other occasions, the staff member dealt with it well and it was the parent who was in the wrong. My action for this situation was to apologise to him. I took responsibility and arranged to meet with him regularly over the next few weeks to check things improved for him and his child. I then privately reviewed the situation with the member of staff, in a spirit of solution-finding improvement.

This approach is particularly important when things don't go right. Owning a mistake and not blaming others is crucial for people to trust you and their relationship with you. All of this is the basis for developing the 'high challenge, low threat' culture that generates improvement that Mary Myatt talks about in her book of the same name [viii].

Intimacy

Trust starts from building a relationship with the person, from being intimate. Building relationships takes time and energy. It can't be done in one meeting or 'get to know you session'. Be prepared to invest.

Use their name when you speak to them and appreciate them. As this builds up you share appropriate personal stories that build connection.

Be genuinely interested in the person. People need to feel loved and valued. They sense insincerity easily. The purpose of building a relationship is to get to know them, not to win them over so that they do as you want them to.

Listening is key, spending time listening to their story and picking up not just on the factual details but on the emotions and responding appropriately. What topic lights up their face? By listening you discover the points of connection that you can make. Steven Covey talks about how highly effective people speak last. They do this because they bring value to the other person by doing so, but also discover points of connection and where to direct their communication energy. Like a good Venn diagram, points of connection are within the intersection. These are common interests, values or goals that you both share. You might not have complete agreement or overlap, but these are the points where you can start conversation, the points you can make links to when sharing vision and values that you want in the organisation.

By modelling elements of honesty and vulnerability ourselves it opens up a 'trust exchange', like a sticker album swap, that allows those following us to feel safe to express theirs. Sometimes this is the foundation stone for building on improvement. They may then ask, "How did you improve things from that situation?"

One of the key features on my desk at work was a box of tissues. I have lost count of the number of times they have been used. When you practise the art of listening, you give others the opportunity to talk. As people face challenges, the pressure can build up and someone listening can 'open the floodgates' allowing them to unload the issues. Metaphorical opening of the floodgates can sometimes lead to the literal floodgates opening as tears flow. I have listened to stories of how people are struggling with bitter divorces, worries about their children who need significant medical care, concern for partners who have been diagnosed with cancer and personal struggles with mental health. And then there are work-based concerns of struggling with workload, disputes with colleagues, how they manage their team and how they handle difficult children and parents. In many of these cases, sharing my equivalent story to find a point of connection was not appropriate. They were times to listen, times to hear the emotions as well as the words and, as a leader, time to evaluate the best way to help them to help themselves.

It is absolutely crucial that you build genuine relationships with people. If your desire is to use a relationship to win a leadership victory or to manipulate people, then it will fail as people quickly detect it is not genuine.

Take Gordon, a leader who had clearly been told by his coach that he had to listen more to those that he worked with and build relationships. And so, he started the next meeting by asking someone's opinion. They shared their thoughts on the issue and told Gordon how it made them feel.

Because Gordon was not genuinely interested in the person; because he was not there to serve them but was there to serve his own position and be viewed as successful; because the person's view did not match his own, he didn't like the answer. "Well, I don't think we will take that line," he said dismissively and quickly then moved on to the targets he wanted the person to meet. Operate like that a few times and you get a reputation for it. It doesn't take long to lose respect when you operate like Gordon.

Building appropriate intimacy with followers, where appropriate personal issues are shared, is key to building relationships that help followers to trust you. But building intimate relationships with fellow leaders helps develop working partnerships that mutually support each other. I had the privilege, in my last ten years of being a headteacher, of networking with a number of similarly experienced headteachers. Two of these, Anna and Shaun, were my closest confidantes. Anna was the one who came to 'hold the fort' in school when most staff and I went to the funeral of a member of staff. Shaun was the headteacher who hosted my whole school of 650 children when we had to evacuate due to a bomb scare and I was 90 miles away at another funeral. But, before the dramatic stories of support, there were years of building trust by sharing stories of how we were doing, risking being vulnerable by expressing the challenges that we were struggling with. None of this was in the context of trying to score points with bigger successes or bigger challenges.

Selflessness

Trust in you as a leader comes when people see that you wish to serve others. Being a leader of the people and for the people and not for your own personal gain is crucial to gain trust. Servant-hearted leadership comes when you listen to those you are leading, understand their position and their emotions and consider these in your decision making.

A good servant leader asks, "What can I do to help you on this journey?" When followers see that the leader is there not to serve themselves, but to bring the best for and out of the people, they will be highly allegiant to the leader. Looking for the win-win where you can in situations ensures that people know you are looking to take people with you.

This is particularly important when making changes. When we looked to bring in a new marking policy at my school, we did the research on what helped learning and presented it to the teachers, outlining new expectations. The change was hard and the ask was big. And so, when some teachers came to see me about the workload increase, I listened carefully. I asked myself what were the key non-negotiables and how I could give concession to the points that they raised. Points that were valid. Points I needed to consider if I was to take them with me and gain some success. Concessions that enabled the improvement to happen and gain some success. But this does not mean that you are soft on things. Being able to tell the hard truths in situations in a solution-focused way shows people that you have a strength that can be relied upon. All of this is the foundation for developing open and honest review of things for improvement, what Matthew Syed calls 'Black Box' thinking. Without developing these things through building strong relationships, it makes it much harder for open and honest review of things.

Crediting ideas to those who generated them and not taking the glory for yourself is another aspect of developing trust. When I was a headteacher, one of the issues we were struggling with was space for breakout small group support. We looked at all sorts of solutions but they were all so expensive. One day, I am sure half-jokingly, one of the teachers, Nic, said, "Why don't you get a double decker bus? There's plenty of room in there." So, after we did the research and we spoke to staff about the idea, I told staff how it came from Nic's original idea.

Expertise

Your credibility as a leader comes in the way that you lead people, in the expertise that you have and the way that you offer that expertise. For the purpose of building trust, it is how we use our expertise that is crucial. Listening to the person, understanding their issue and then offering them advice if they would like to take it, enables the follower to see that you are person-centred and not self-centred. My role as leadership development coach and trainer means that I meet regularly with education and business leaders. As a coach, I am trained to listen to the person and instead of giving my opinion, my answer, I ask a series of questions to help them discover a solution. Occasionally, they need help. At this point I ask their permission to offer an idea. I say to them, "I have something that might be helpful to you. Would you like me to share it with you to consider?" They have nearly always said yes to this and I make it clear that they are free to use it or ignore it. A good leader lifts people up to achieve higher standards. The spirit of care and improvement drives their expertise-sharing.

Another key factor of trust is having the honesty of knowing the limits of your experience and being able to say, "I can't help you there but I will find someone who perhaps can," and following through with it.

The table below summarises the 5 key ways to build trust.

Authenticity	Reliability	Intimacy	Selflessness	Expertise
Honesty Integrity Responsibility Credit people	**Expectation Deliverer**	**Listener Appreciative Personable relational**	**Listen Win-win Hard truths**	**Expert Adviser**
You tell the truth and do the right thing. You give credit to the person and take responsibility for solving problems.	You want to do the best you can and when you promise to do something you make sure it happens.	You are people-focused. You listen to what they want and build relationships by using their name and remembering important details.	You listen to understand not to hold a conversation. You look to find a solution that works for everyone. If you need to tell a hard truth you do it with care for the person.	You take your job seriously and learn all that you can. You have developed an expertise in your field and you offer good advice based on what they need.

Purpose of relationships

Some may be asking why build relationships? Why worry about 'affiliative' leadership style when you can have the 'coercive' style of just telling people what to do? Well firstly, the coercive style needs to be used carefully. It is great when there is a fire alarm and you are just telling people to get out of the building. But use it too often and you become a tyrant and disengage your staff. Ruling by fear means that you are not really the king or queen of the kingdom. You are only truly king or queen when people willingly bow to the knee, not when they are forced to. *You may have the crown and own the land but the people no longer follow you. The kingdom is the people!*

Consider anything that you have become involved in. Maybe a hobby, a faith group, a club you belong to or maybe your job. There may be a range of reasons that you joined, but what has kept you involved? It is likely that the group manifesto aligns with your views, beliefs or principles, but a key factor that keeps people involved is where they develop relationships with those in the group. Relationships keep people engaged, particularly through any difficulty the group faces.

The affiliative style builds relationships with people so they understand you as a person, and trust your motives. On its own it may struggle to get high level development in an organisation, particularly with some personality types. However, it is a great foundation for the 'authoritative' and 'coaching' styles which help to gain movement in people's thinking and practice.

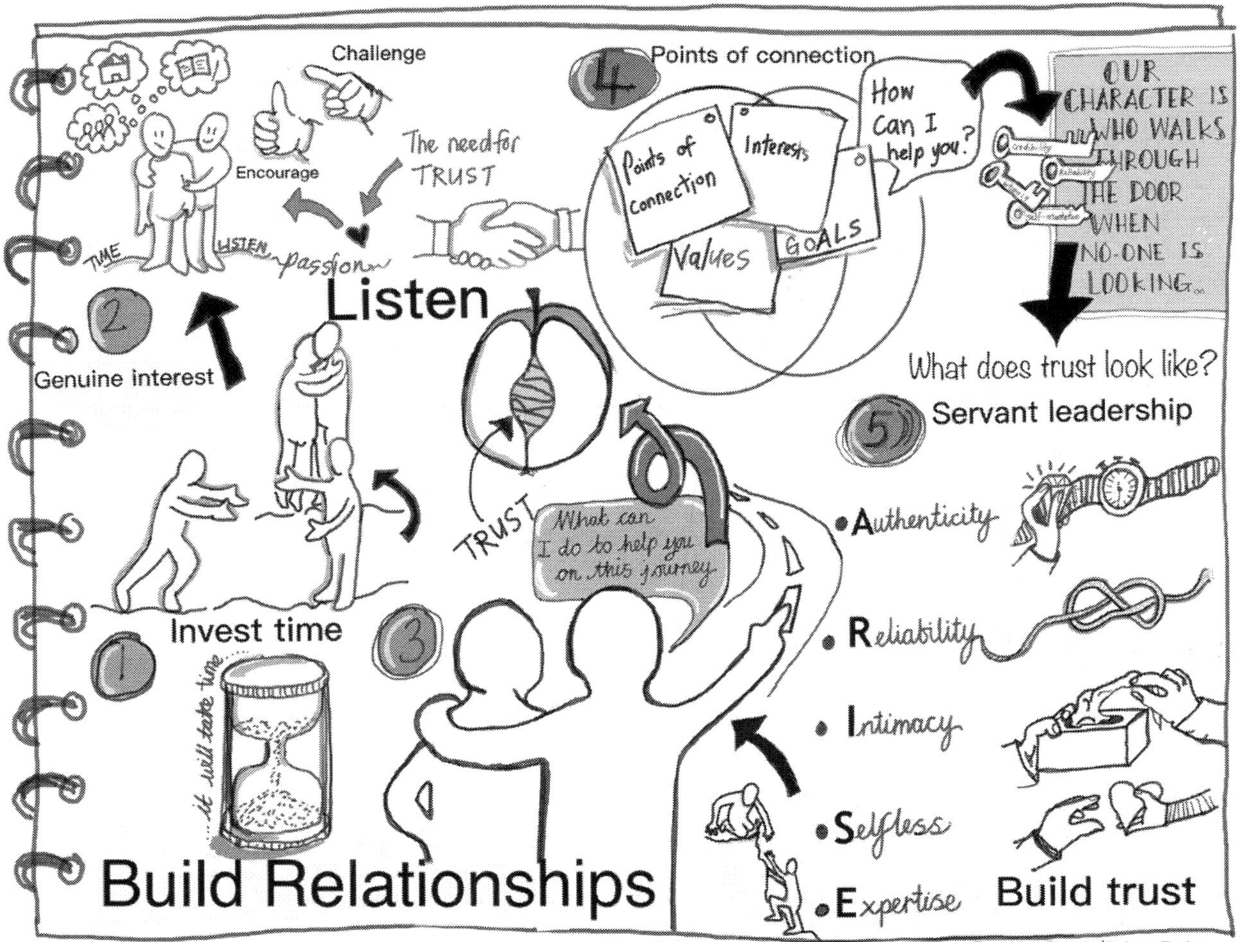

©Everyday People/© Jane Ryder

Personal Reflection – Build Relationships

Trust			
How do I develop trust? RAG (Red, Amber, Green) how you use them.			
ARISE		RAG	How I can develop
Authenticity	Honesty		
	Integrity		
	Responsibility		
	Credit people		
Reliability	Expectation		
	Listener		

Personal Reflection – Build Relationships

Trust			
ARISE		RAG	How I can develop
Intimacy	Intimacy – listener		
	Intimacy – appreciative		
	Personable		
	Relation		
Selflessness	Listen		
	Win-win		
	Hard truths		
Expertise	Expert		
	Adviser		

Chapter 4: Develop Others

Cyril, Doc and Paul

"Put simply, if you can empower others to lead, you have more of you leading, which spreads the load. But leadership also has a far higher moral purpose. Good leaders lift people up, empowering them to know their direction and what story they want to write. When we give people time and develop them, we firstly help them see they have value. When we accept them for who they are, recognise their strengths and help them build their capacity to lead, we empower them to bring value to others and so the cycle continues. Life without purpose is fruitless. Life with purpose generates purpose in others."

Uncool but so cool

If you were to pick a role model for a group of teenage boys, you would perhaps be tempted to look for style, a cool outfit or maybe sporting prowess. But I learnt early on that these are superficial add-ons. What really matters is valuing people and seeking to help them discover who they could be. Cyril Wearn, my 1980s youth leader, did not have cool clothes or sporting prowess. His job was not cool for teenage lads; he was manager of a Boots store and a Justice of the Peace. But what he was amazing at was developing and mentoring. I'd been part of Cyril's church youth group for a couple of years. Sundays were ok, but what we really loved were Friday club nights. Snooker, table tennis, fizzy pop in glass bottles for 20p and packets of crisps for 5p. Occasionally, all of us would all pile into Cyril's seven-seater Peugeot 504 estate to go out for a night-time game of 'hunt the flag' or a trip out. There were also camping trips for the weekend. Underpinning all of this was Cyril building relationships with the young lads in his care, encouraging us, celebrating who we were, instilling healthy competition and aspiration. Shepherding us, guiding us in good moral character. It is not just the rose-coloured glasses of older age that distil awe and respect for Cyril. As teenage lads, we had ultimate respect for him and we learnt an early lesson: that respect was not generated by clothing or position. It was earned by investing in and developing people. If you are going to be purposeful in developing others, it comes in four parts:

- A relationship opens the door
- Purposeful mentoring develops the character
- Planned opportunities root the practice
- Review & planning develop excellence

A relationship opens the door

As I look back on this, what Cyril seemed to know was that developing others starts with building a relationship. Chapter 3 has covered this in detail. By building a relationship, you learn about the person's history, their values, what makes them tick. In turn, it enables you to encourage and to challenge them in such a way that the words 'speak into their life', taking hold and shaping them.

As a young lad, my family was relatively poor. As I look back as an adult, I am amazed how mum and dad managed financially to support three strapping lads. But, as a 14-year-old, my understanding of family economics was not quite so developed, and one thing that really frustrated me was that while everyone else in my friendship circle had modern Ford Cortinas or Vauxhall Cavaliers, we had a 1965 Sunbeam Rapier. It was a 1960s car in poo brown and we were in the 1980s; it was a source of embarrassment, and to me seemed to broadcast to everyone, 'We're poor.' It was also the source of a sore bottom due to an extremely uncomfortable rear seat, and one Sunday it was my turn to sit in it. But not today. I made my stand and refused to travel in it, choosing instead to walk home the 2 miles from church. And it was Cyril who drove past me, stopped, wound down the window and told me to jump in. He knew what had been said, he knew the stand I was taking. And because he was a wise man who invested in us lads, he listened, he understood and then as he dropped me off, kindly challenged me, reminding me of the sacrifices my parents were making and suggested that maybe I should ease up on them. He earned the right to challenge, through painstaking hours of building a relationship and trust. As a result, he developed my thinking that day.

Purposeful mentoring develops character

The concept of purposeful mentoring is not a new one. Now they might not have used the term mentoring, but back in the 4th Century BC, Greek philosophers Socrates, Aristotle and Plato had disciples. They chose people to spend time with them, debate with them, watch their every movement. Helping them develop the thinking and skills needed. The same principle was seen 400 years later with Jesus with his twelve disciples. In the Bible accounts, you will see the disciples spending time with Jesus, hearing how he taught people, watching how he dealt with people. In time, the disciples learnt every aspect of the character of their leader in order to graft it into their own. Now, I certainly don't recommend mentoring as many as twelve people who directly report to you. But although modern mentoring does not involve spending 24 hours a day with each other like the ancient disciples, it still has that purposeful development of others as a core principle.

I first met Paul Wilcox in the 1990s, when he was director of Covenanters. Covenanters was a youth organisation providing resources to churches to support the spiritual and moral development of young people. What struck me, on first meeting Paul, was how accessible he was. Despite being the national director of something, he was not aloof or self-important. He was friendly, he listened, was thoughtful and had a sense of humour. Paul believed passionately in mentoring and developing young people. This was ideally suited to leading an organisation like Covenanters. But Paul did not just talk about it or encourage others to do it. He modelled it. Paul would take young leaders that he knew and invite them to travel with him, attend meetings with him and, like the early Greek disciples, to watch how he dealt with things and then unpick with them what they saw. They could see how he dealt with difficult people, how he dealt with problems, how his beliefs and values drove decisions and how they wrestled with challenges.

That purposeful mentoring not only taught them skills but allowed them to see how your thoughts, feelings and actions shape your character. So passionate was he about developing people that when he left Covenanters, he established The Mentor Network, an organisation to connect mentors and those needing mentoring.

I have never been privileged to have received purposeful development in my career. But I have made sure that I have given time to this for others in my leadership. I would love to have done it for everyone, but this is not possible as you cannot give the time and energy to it. The trick is to do well for a few what you would love to do for everyone.

Gemma Smith was an outstanding young teacher. She had a thorough curriculum knowledge, engaged children in learning and was a positive, solution-focused person. She had been a curriculum leader for Maths and English but I could see in her someone who was capable of leading even more. She could, if she wanted to, become an outstanding headteacher. She didn't lack confidence; she was a balanced person. But she couldn't see what we could see; her amazing potential. So I called it. One day I invite her to my office for a chat. She knocked, smiled through the inspection window in the door, and entered on my nod and beckoning wave. She looked a little worried, concerned as to why she was asked to come to the headteacher's office. I sensed this and quickly got to the point to allay any fears she had and spoke to her. "Gemma, you are a tremendous member of staff. You are positive, supportive, teach confidently and lead well. I am so glad you are on staff here. I can see, though, that you are even more capable and I would like to meet up with you every couple of weeks and mentor you so that you are confident to apply for any senior leadership positions that come up."

She looked both shocked and pleased as the offer sank in. I gave her time to think about it and she returned a couple of days later, thanked me for the offer and was keen to take it up. Over the next three months we met every three weeks and worked through a leadership book, discussing what she had found useful, how she had put it into practice and the challenges she had found. She was a joy to work with, highly reflective and conscientious and developed in confidence in her leadership ability. After four months she applied for an Assistant Headteacher post and was successful. The formal mentoring then stopped, but continued informally as she did the role, when she would pop in for a chat over a cuppa.

Process of purposeful mentoring

So how do you go about purposeful mentoring? I think it goes through the following stages:

- Identify the person
- Call it
- Invite to develop
- Clear process & timescale
- Mentor & coach
- Opportunities
- No-blame culture

Identify the person

You are not looking for a lifetime disciple. The idea is that you will walk with them for a time helping them develop in an identified area. It could be someone you see has potential. They may be stuck and need that boost to get over a hurdle. It is likely to be someone that you see as receptive. It is likely to be someone you know will benefit from your particular experience.

Call it

This is the first part of approaching the person. 'Calling it' is about expressing what you see in them – the talent they have, the potential they have – and identifying that you see mentoring would be good for them and that you would like to develop them.

Invite to develop

Being mentored has to be entered into willingly. It may be that it is not the right time for them, with other external issues. It may be that they don't identify with you. Forcing someone to be mentored will not be successful. So invite them. Give them time to think about it.

Clear process & timescale

Explain how you see it happening and the sort of timescale you envisage. For example, is it a once a week meeting? Is it a book club style, where you read a leadership book together? Will it be attending things with you and then debriefing? How long is it for each week and over how many weeks or months? This is something to be mutually discussed that works for you both.

Mentor & Coach

You will work with a range of people. Some will be self-learners and will pick things up quickly. Others will need much more explicit explanation. You will need to adapt your style with each person. Mentoring is where you share your experience to help develop them. Coaching is where you use questioning to draw out their thinking.

In my experience, starting from the person's area of interest and the issue they need to improve on, and using a blend of both coaching and mentoring, brings deep learning in their development as a leader.

Opportunities

Watching you lead and unpicking it is helpful. Where rich learning happens is when they try putting it into practice for themselves. The process that you want to take people through is:

- I do, you watch
- I do, you help
- You do, I help
- You do, I watch

Planning opportunities for them to try out what they have learnt allows them to gain confidence.

No-blame culture

Any sense of threat reduces creative thinking. Creating a sense where it is ok to get things wrong, providing there is willingness to learn and develop, ensures people can own the improvement.

Planned opportunities root the practice

Doc Holliday was head of PE at Glebelands School in Cranleigh. He was calm, assured and respected by all of the lads. He didn't need to shout, be aggressive or use pressure. He just didn't allow you to get away with things but treated people with the respect that he expected you to give him and to give yourself. None of us ever asked what his first name really was, he was just Doc Holliday.

Like all PE teachers he gave time to extra-curricular PE and encouraged you to find your niche. Rugby and athletics were mine. Doc Holliday oversaw the athletics team at school and encouraged me as I developed at hurdles and became district champion. I loved my rugby; being a large lad I found my niche playing for the school team, encouraged by Derek Coward, the other PE teacher. One day, as I walked through the PE department corridor past Doc Holliday's office, he called me over. I wonder if Doc Holliday knew the impact his question would have. "Colin, I know you like your rugby, and I wondered if you would like to help me train the Y7 rugby team?" Maybe his reason for asking was just because he needed a bit of help? He didn't need help with any other team he ran, he was quite competent! I never asked him, but I like to think that he saw in me some potential for leading and working with children. I did help him with the year 7 team. I have no recollection of any ground breaking achievement with that team, but what I do know is that purposeful opportunity presented to me by Doc Holliday was one of three key moments that changed my mind about working with children and started me off on a career in education that lasted nearly 30 years.

The second of those key moments was presented to me by Cyril Wearn. As you know from earlier in the chapter, Cyril invested in us as a group of lads. Cyril's greatest investment in me was when he asked me one day to help with running the 'Adventurers'. Now the title sounds grand, but in reality it was running the 7-11 age group at church. Six excitable 7-11-year-olds. It would send most people running off in a frenzy, which is probably why Cyril was asking me!
My memory was that Cyril followed the same mentoring process that I mentioned above.

- I do, you watch
- I do, you help
- You do, I help
- You do, I watch

He gave me time to just watch him, then gradually gave me little things to help with. In time, he said, "Why don't you have a go at leading this part?" and then gradually increased what I did.

Now you could be forgiven for thinking this approach is just good for teenagers. But it is a key part of mentoring in the workplace. The best training and development is a blended mixture of training, coaching, mentoring, planned experience and constructive debrief.

If I am honest, I don't think I ever quite got performance management with staff right throughout my schools. However hard I tried, it was still seen by some as a 'doing it to me' rather than person-driven. But the very best approach I discovered was when there was a coaching relationship. Coaching the individual to identify their area for development, targeting the learning and experience that improved it, and reviewing success saw the most engagement and progress.

When working with Gemma, we talked about the theory and what it would look like in practice, and then Gemma would try it out. "Gemma, there is a staff training session coming up in 3 weeks. I would like you to lead it, putting into practice the things we have looked at. We will then debrief on it afterwards." She had run some before, so some of this was not new, but she was approaching it in a different context and practising some of the theory around working with people.

Sometimes those planned opportunities need support. Emma was a science graduate and a lovely, calm teacher. I had seen her grow in confidence since she joined us and the post of science leader had come up. I spoke to her about it, and she loved the idea, but was nervous. Having that ability to just sense when is the time to push, when is the time to pull back and when is the time to provide support is important. I sensed now was the time to provide support.

So I arranged for a highly experienced and incredibly efficient senior leader to work alongside her and mentor her for a while. Emma had seen enough examples of how to lead. In her case she needed to do it, but needed someone walking alongside helping her in the initial stages. This worked well and before long Emma was running science; she developed a great science day and rewrote parts of the curriculum. She gathered evidence and a year later the school was awarded a chartermark of the Silver Science Award.

Review & planning roots excellence

There are many athletes who train hard, but not all of them achieve success. Thinking over the last 20 years has moved away from the 'natural born talent' view of what makes you a champion and has moved towards a growth mindset approach. Anyone can achieve in an area if they practise enough. Malcolm Gladwell suggested that 10,000 hours of practice is what makes you talented in an area, although that theory is now much debated. Matthew Syed's book, Bounce[ix], talks about the impact of practice. One of the key things to remember though, is it is not the practice alone that makes you champion at something. It is what you practise on and the feedback you receive. Key to this is a good coach – someone who helps you unpick what is working well and what could be even better, and how to hone that area.

It is the same with developing others. Reviewing how their planned opportunity went and then planning development from it is crucial. A key to this is the starting point. Start with appreciative thinking.

Appreciative thinking

There is real power from starting from the positive. It is not just a nicety or something that kind people do. When you review things with someone, for a range of reasons it can be stressful. When we get stressed the brain releases a hormone called Cortisol. This negatively affects the prefrontal cortex part of the brain. This is where planning, complex cognitive behaviour, personality expression, decision making, and moderating social behaviour takes place. High and prolonged stress affects our ability to process thoughts and behaviours and create memory. [x] Research by Emmons & McCulloch in 2003 [xi] shows that when you start from a position of thankfulness it releases hormones DHEA and DHEA-S [xii]. This has the ability to counteract and lower cortisol, thus allowing the brain to utilise cognitive thought to think more constructively.

Appreciative thinking works on the principle of 1) what worked well and 2) what could be even better? By starting the review with what works well, it is positive and thankful and reduces stress to allow an openness to examine the negative, and constructively think of ways to improve.

Focusing on the right things

One aspect of my leadership development work is coaching. As a coach, I work through a series of questions in order to help the person discover the root of their issue. People start with what they think is the issue, but often it sits far deeper.

In November 2018, I was asked by a school academy trust of pupil referral units to visit one of the schools to analyse what was going on and what could be done to help the school. Pupil referral units are for children who have struggled to access mainstream education, and resulting behaviours impact on their ability to learn.

As I visited the school, on the surface, the obvious issue was that poor behaviour in the children was hindering learning. But to focus on the right things you have to dig deeper; you need to ask the right question. What is causing this? The obvious answers to that was a) there was not a consistent approach to managing behaviour, b) the curriculum was poor and disengaging children and c) staff needed training in both these areas. But, to focus on the right thing, you have to dig deeper. The school had gone through a 66% change in its leadership and a 50% change in staffing. There had been a high influx of high-need children. All of these were contributing winds to the whirlwind the school found itself in, but they were still not the root cause and the thing that needed to be focused on first. Why was there not a consistent approach to behaviour or a curriculum that engaged pupils?

At the root of all the issues was that the school had lost sight of its purpose and lacked a clear belief in the process that would develop the children (its 'transformation theory'). The leadership was not clear on this and therefore the staff and children certainly couldn't be. The school was asked to focus on:

- What is our purpose?
- What is our theory of transformation or change? How will we help children get there? What is it that we do that helps them?

When the school knew the answer to these questions then it would drive a) what the curriculum would look like and b) what the approach to behaviour would be, to help pupils develop.

When you know your 'why', you walk in and towards your purpose. When you know your 'why' it makes your 'how' and 'what' more engaging. So, that was the starting point. I helped them narrow their transformation theory down to:

Know What do we know about the child? What works for them? What is a bad trigger for them?

Show We model the behaviours. We show them in a curriculum what it means to be empowered for good choices.

Grow Empowerment is the key for them to take responsibility. We therefore give them two choices when their behaviour is poor. We create a curriculum that engages and that they can pose questions in and explore.

By focusing on the core issue of establishing a clear purpose, it engages staff in a common goal. When things are tough, they continue to work hard at it as they know what they are aiming for. In this case, by knowing the core purpose, it drives a curriculum and behaviour management system that fit that goal. There is purpose and reason to what is being done.

So how do you focus on the right things and not stop too early at the most apparent? It basically comes down to the simple fact of asking the following questions.

"What is happening?" Say what you see.

"What might be causing that?" This often falls into the following categories:

Purpose Is the purpose clear in the leader? Is it clear in the people? Is it modelled? Is it constantly part of the agenda of the organisation? What evidence do I see of this?

People Are the right people on the team? Are they in the right positions? When people are not engaging, the problem comes down to either 'skill' or 'will' or both. Are they skilled in what needs to be done? Or is it their will, in that they do not share the vision for the organisation and are 'poisoning the well'? Maybe it is a combination of both, in that they neither share the vision nor have the skills to effectively talk about areas of conflict.

Position Is it something organisational that is hindering the progress of the vision? Has the vision changed but the systems stayed as before and so don't support the vision?

If it is an individual that you are helping to find the root cause to focus on, there are similar issues:

Purpose Are they clear on their purpose?

People Is it a people-related issue? Help them to focus on their behaviours and what they can control rather than on what they can't control (eg, the other person's behaviour).

Position Is it something organisational that they are faced with? Again, help them to focus on what is in their control.

Developing others is a key part of leadership

One of the greatest achievements for me is the number of people in leadership who used to work for me. In its simplest form, if you can empower others to lead, you have more of you leading, spreading the load. But it also has a far higher moral purpose. Good leaders lift people up, empowering them to know their purpose and what story they want to write. When we give people time and develop them, we firstly help them see they have value. When we accept them for who they are and recognise their strengths and help them build their capacity to lead we empower them to bring value to others and therefore give them purpose. Life without purpose is fruitless. Life with purpose germinates purpose in others.

PURPOSEFUL
Earn the right to challenge
Do it well with a few
I do, you watch
I do, you help
You do, I help
You do, I watch
IDENTIFY WHO
Review and plan for excellence
purposeful mentoring develops the character
planned opportunities root the practice
Relationship opens the door
stay connected
Purpose ✓
People ✓
Review ✓
Develop Others
© Everyday People/©Jane Ryder

Personal Reflection – Develop Others

Mentor	
Have you been lucky enough for someone to mentor or develop you? Reflect on times when people have mentored you. What did you find helpful?	
What was helpful?	What was not so helpful?

Pass it forward
Who could you mentor? What could you offer them? Work your way through the process.
Identify: Who could you mentor?
Call it: What do you see in them?
Invite to develop: Have you developed a trust relationship with them?

Personal Reflection – Develop Others

Purposeful Mentoring
Mentor & Coach: What area of expertise could you offer them?
Opportunities: What experiences could you offer them?
No Blame Culture: Are you prepared for them to make mistakes?

Relationship		
If you are working with someone, review yourself against the 4 key areas.		
Area	Score/10	Reflection
Relationships open the door		
Purposeful mentoring develops character		
Planned opportunities root the practice		
Review & Plan develops excellence		

Chapter 5: Have Integrity

Simon and Dave

"Integrity is a key part of real, natural authority. A person's integrity, gained through moral purpose and experience that gives assurance, helps them to be credible. Honest, consistent respect of others then builds that deep, visceral, instinctive connection and trust. When you mix this with the drive to serve those around you, that is when it prompts actions from others as they buy in not only to the manifesto, but you as a person."

Under pressure

I admired Simon Phillips from the moment I met him. His genuine warmth, compassion and deep sense of calm was always present. As a headteacher, this was a tremendous asset, especially as his schools served many families where that sense of calm was exactly what was needed. Whenever we met, he would share challenges that he was facing, but always with a sense of composure, of forward thinking. Simon and his family also fostered children. You couldn't fail to like Simon. He is just one of life's lovely people. So when the mobile rang that day and I saw it was Simon's number, I picked it up looking forward to catching up with him.

"Colin, can we meet up?" He was calm and gentle in manner, yet there was something about the tone, a slight inflection, that just told me this was not the normal phone call.

"Of course we can. Are you ok?" I queried.

"They want me to go. Can you come to the house to chat?"

If you have ever been 'let go' or 'asked to leave' or 'left for personal reasons' or 'put under pressure to leave' or sacked, you will know the complete devastation that you can feel. You will know the sense of failure, loneliness. You will know the dread of even going to the local supermarket, fearing what others have been told or mis-told about your departure and therefore might confront you. It is in those moments that a range of emotions can flood in. It begins initially with being stunned, it moves to sadness, then fear, then anger. Sometimes they all come at once or play a game of tag wrestling with your mind, taking turns. But unlike a wrestler, they show no mercy, even when you slam the floor with your hand and shout, "I yield."

So as I walked down the path to see Simon with another headteacher friend, we wondered which Simon we would see. He greeted us. Admittedly slightly tender and bruised, but he was still the same balanced, thoughtful man we knew. His job had ended, but he would not allow it to take, bend or warp who he was. Simon remained Simon.

The dictionary definition of integrity means 'the quality of being honest and having strong moral principles'. In engineering, integrity has a particular meaning that is so helpful for us to understand the integrity needed as a leader. When building or machining something, the product needs 'structural integrity'. **Structural integrity** is the ability of an item – either a structural component or a structure consisting of many components – to hold together under a load, including its own weight, without breaking or deforming excessively. In other words, even under pressure it remains firm, resolute, unchanged.

Now of course, Simon shared the sadness he felt and all of the emotions I described above. But underneath all of that, he did not allow bitterness to change the shape of who he was. He did not allow anger to change the way he spoke. Even under pressure his core structure and integrity remained intact.

And so, years later, when I experienced job loss, he was one of the first I called to ask for advice, so that I could model the same integrity under pressure that he modelled.

Moral fibre

Integrity is essentially about a person's character. Character is not something you are born with or you just copy. Character starts with our thinking. The work of Emerging Leaders, in their Leadership for Life programme[xiii], teaches that our character starts with our thinking. The process that shapes our character is below.

So the character is built up over time and what it becomes is based on either the positive or negative thinking that you put into it.

So how do you know whether a thought and action or a decision you are about to take is something that will contribute towards a character of integrity? On my keyring, I have six beads. On each bead is a letter that acts as an acrostic to help judge any decision.

T, N, R, P, L, A

These six letters help me consider whether my action can be considered as **True, Noble, Right, Pure, Lovely** and **Admirable**. If you don't want a key ring or can't remember 6 words, then ask yourself, "Will this lift people up or will it push people down?"

It doesn't matter if anyone is looking, or if the action becomes public. Remember, your character is who walks through the door when no-one is looking. Another way of looking at the decision, although slightly more cynical, is: "How will it look if it appears in the press?" An example of this is Blake Mycoskie. While travelling in Argentina in 2006, Blake witnessed the hardships faced by children growing up without shoes. His solution to the problem was simple, yet revolutionary: to create a for-profit business that made shoes – TOMS (Tomorrow's shoes). When you bought a pair of his shoes, they donated a pair to a child in need. Since 2006 TOMS has donated over 60 million pairs of shoes. It's a story, a belief, a manifesto that has captured the hearts of millions of people as they were not just buying the quality of the shoes, but the quality of the vision to respond to a clear need. Both Blake and the millions of shoe buyers were driven by the need of those 60 million children's feet that needed shoes.

Developing integrity is an internal process. It is like a muscle and needs to be exercised, practised daily. It comes down to 4 core elements:

- moral purpose
- a clear manifesto for improvement
- an assurance and conviction based on experience
- wisdom through listening

Manifesto

Recently, on social media, I came across a former pupil of the first school I taught at, The Duke of Kent School. Dave Cornthwaite is an English adventurer, writer, filmmaker and founder of the 'YesTribe'. I also remember him as a delightful former pupil.

As I read information on his social media site, I was intrigued by the man he has become and the 'YesTribe' that he has established. Dave, on his website www.sayyesmore.com, explains the purpose of the 'YesTribe'.

"We live in a society riddled with expectations and life can sometimes seem harder than ever. Stress and a call to work long hours is at odds with the pressure we feel to live picture (social media)-perfect lives, and the solution to many mental health issues which is right on our doorstep. Based around forming strong face-to-face communities and the power of spending time in nature, SayYesMore.com is an affirmation that habitually saying yes is a sure-fire foundation of a kind, happy and enjoyable life, and a reminder during our hardest times that we're always capable of more. Every time we do something new we grow, so not being afraid to fail and making the most of every day means we have to grasp opportunities when they come along, and our basic message is that in any given moment we can choose positive or negative, and that small positive lifestyle changes make a big difference."

When you read on you discover how the members of 'YesTribe' have raised over £750,000 for good causes in the last year and have travelled well over 100,000 miles on human-powered journeys. They have an annual microfestival for positive change called Yestival, weekly free campouts where they wild camp under the stars. They have even converted a former London double-decker bus into a solar powered community hub where ideas are encouraged towards reality.

Seth Godin, in his book Tribes [xiv], explains that at the start of a tribe is an important manifesto, which people can connect to. Dave has that manifesto, of freedom, liberation and of social change. It brings integrity to the leader, when the purpose is not for the benefit of the leader, but for the benefit of those the manifesto seeks to serve.

Spend some time looking through the sayyesmore.com website and it is obvious that Dave's leadership has integrity. His manifesto has purpose and is about positive change. And his heart is for others, helping 'adventure' become accessible for all and creating a community that serves others in the process.

Assurance, experience, conviction

"Dad," said the little voice at the end of the phone, "you need to come quick to help mummy. She can't speak." As it turned out, Mummy really couldn't speak. She had yawned whilst waiting in a doctor's surgery and had dislocated her jaw, leaving it locked open. Perhaps a good place for this to happen, but nevertheless she was in immense pain and she still needed to be taken to hospital to have it reset. As the nearest A&E department did not have the right consultant available, it was a long, but quiet journey to the next hospital that did. After several failed attempts from the A&E doctor there, the consultant was called for. His arrival was signalled by a sense of calm proceeding him as he gently walked up the corridor. "Now my dear, I know this is painful, but it will all be over very soon." He calmly explained to the doctor the method he was going to try, and went behind my wife to start the procedure. The A&E doctor tried to justify the approach he had taken, to which the consultant politely replied in a nurturing tone, "Yes, I know the book says that, but this is what works." With what seemed like magician hands, gently massaging the jaw, my wife's jaw was back in place, as tears of relief trickled down her face.

I continue to have immense respect for all members of our NHS. They minister to people bringing daily relief to people. They all deserve a medal every day. The consultant in this story demonstrated the role of a leader with integrity as he spoke with assurance, experience and conviction. They have done these sorts of things before, in different contexts; they have tested the extremes beyond the book and manual.

They know it will work, not just in their head, but in their heart and from experience and so can speak with authority: "This will work - come with me." What I loved about that consultant is that he not only reassured my wife, but after putting the jaw back in place he reassured his junior doctor and pastorally taught him. He saw himself as an elder, sharing his wisdom to benefit the next generation of doctors and patients who would not even be in his presence. He was driven by the need of the patient and the junior doctor, not by a personal need to elevate himself. His elevation came through elevating others.

In moments like these, speaking with assurance is obvious, but how do you show it when you are in a group, sharing ideas? How do you work on generating assurance and authority when someone has not got it all right? It works like this. Someone has shared their view. Someone else, with experience and knowledge in this area, understands that large parts of their idea won't work well. Someone with integrity does not dismiss all of the first person's idea. They include the good part of it to engage them. Successful and wise engagement happens by the following approach:

1. Respect the valid part of the idea already expressed.
2. Explain your good idea encompassing the good part of the first person's idea.
3. Explain the 'why' or purpose of your good idea.
4. Give an example or story of how it has worked before.
5. Explain the impact it has had in the past and could have in this situation.

And all of this is in the same spirit that the medical consultant demonstrated. It is to elevate and encourage and develop others, not for the purpose of elevating yourself. By recognising the other person's starting point and strength, you help them grow and develop.

Wisdom

History books and religious stories talk of sages - wise men and women who had the ability to have insight in a decision. Now, think of all those you have met. Have you seen wisdom? I have seen it. When you meet a person with real wisdom, you will notice that they all have one key attribute. Steven Covey talks about it in Highly Effective Habit 5[xv], when he says, "Seek first to understand." Simon Sinek talks about it in even simpler terms: "Speak last." At the root of both of these is the ability to listen first and then speak. By listening first, you can gain a complete understanding of the person and what they are saying. You can then direct your energies in speaking to address the gap and move thinking on.

Integrity – key component to real authority

Integrity is a key part of real, natural authority. A person's integrity, gained through moral purpose and experience that gives assurance, helps them to be credible. Honest, consistent respect of others then builds that deep, visceral, instinctive connection and trust. When you mix this with the drive to those around you, that is when it prompts actions from others as they buy in not only to the manifesto but you as a person.

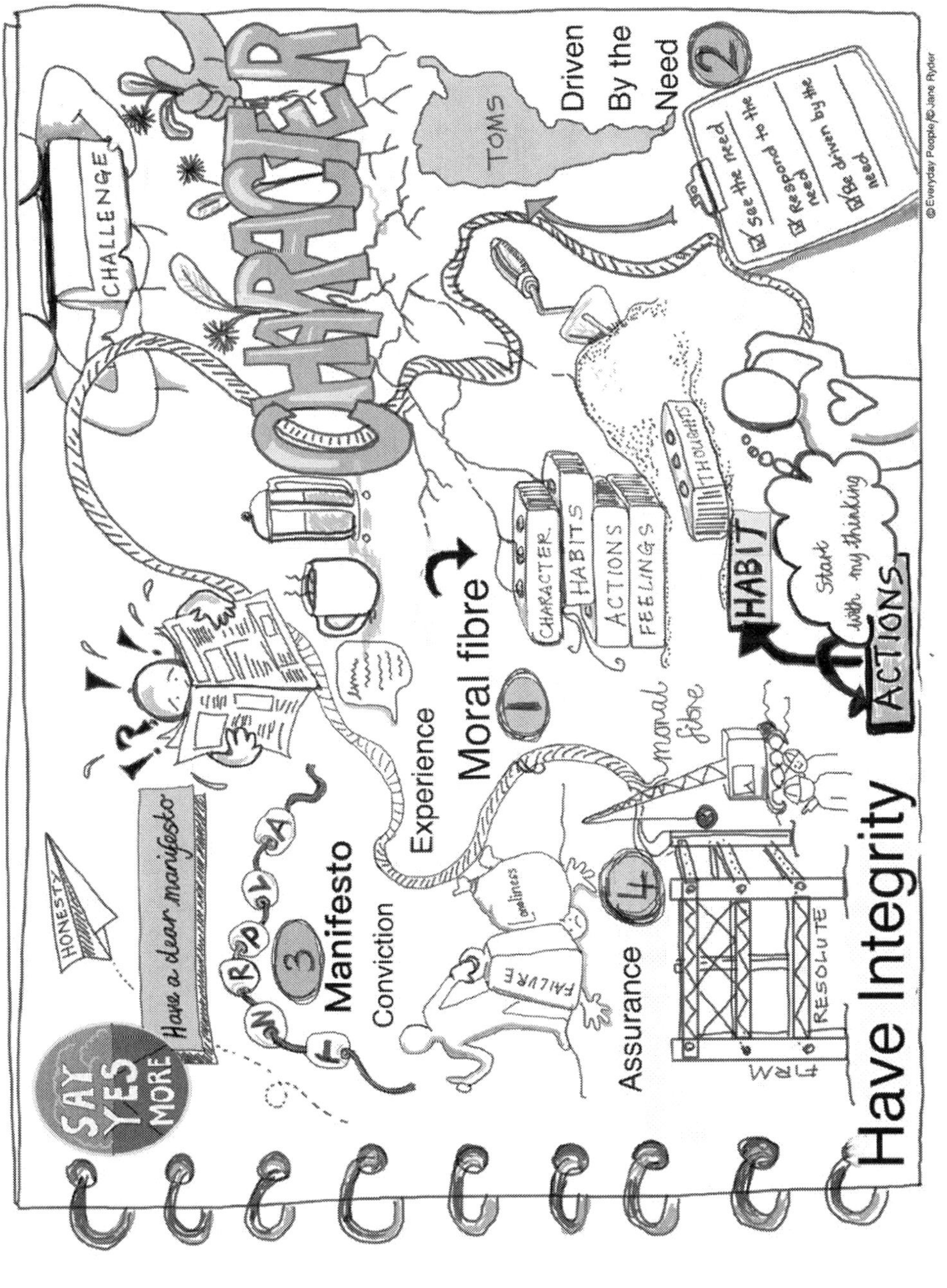

SAY YES MORE
Have a clear manifesto
HONESTY
3
Manifesto
Conviction
Experience
Moral fibre
1
Assurance
FAILURE
loneliness
4
FIRM
RESOLUTE
moral fibre
Have Integrity
CHARACTER
HABITS
ACTIONS
FEELINGS
THOUGHTS
HABIT
Start with my thinking
ACTIONS
CHALLENGE
CHARACTER
TOMS
Driven By the Need
2
See the need
Respond to the need
Be driven by the need
© Everyday People/© Jane Ryder

Personal Reflection – Integrity

TNRPLA
What is your character like? Do you make decisions that are True, Noble, Right, Pure, Lovely and Admirable? Review your last week – how was your decision making?
What is it like under pressure? Does it have structural integrity?
Ask a colleague about your character. What do they say about you?

Personal Reflection – Integrity

Integrity		
Score yourself on the elements of integrity. RAG (Red, Amber, Green)		
Inspire items	RAG	Action
Manifesto for others		
Consistent		
Experience in different contexts		
Speak last & respect other's view		
Appreciate others		
Credit others		
Develop others		

Thoughts, feelings, actions, habits, character
Reflect on your thinking this week. Are there areas that have become a habit (good or bad)? What do you need to change thinking on?

Chapter 6: Communicate Powerfully

Dave & Miranda, Nick & Annette,

Rae and Hannah

"Dissonance in message and reality creates dissonance in how people accept the message. To communicate powerfully you need to have authenticity. What you say from your mouth must be matched by the actions that you then take."

He stopped, paused for dramatic effect, turned and looked into the camera. Time seemed to stand still as he held his gaze. And in that moment you were convinced, sold.

This is the movie image of a powerful communicator. Slick, purposeful and a great orator using their voice, body and mannerisms to full effect to sell the idea. Is that what powerful communication is all about?

In my time, I have heard a number of speakers like this, whose acting talents and voice purvey their message. They are technically very good and tick all the communication boxes. As a leader we can perhaps be tempted to think that this is what we should aspire to be when communicating. But in my experience, if this is all that we rely on as a leader we have missed an important aspect. As a leader, all communication must have one key ingredient if it will have success.

Communication dissonance - lack of authenticity

In language we have something called an oxymoron. An oxymoron is a figure of speech in which apparently contradictory terms appear simultaneously. Phrases like 'act naturally', 'conspicuous absence', 'cruel kindness', 'deceptively honest' and 'openly deceptive' are examples of oxymorons. Oxymorons hold a dissonance. Dissonance is when there is a lack of harmony or synchronicity between two things. For example, 'openly deceptive', how can you be both open and deceptive? Dissonance, scientifically and musically, is where two sound waves are not in synchronicity but are 'out of sync' and therefore not in harmony and cause jarring in our mind as we hear the sounds. An uncomfortable experience and we don't want to hear any more.

For communication to be powerful and truly effective as a leader, it needs to not only have well-crafted words, actions, mannerisms and orator skills. It needs to have authenticity. Authenticity is where there is harmony between words and actions. Without authenticity sitting right at the heart of any communication, you are left with what I will call communication dissonance. The words say one thing, but the actions, whether seen or unseen, tell a different story.

So let's take Desmond, for example. Desmond is a leader in a charitable setting. He's technically a very good speaker. He can stand in front of large audiences week in, week out speaking passionately and confidently on the vision for the organisation. But yet when it comes to attending events that he calls others to attend, he is rarely seen. When it comes to modelling the honesty and integrity to his colleagues that he calls others to demonstrate, it is rarely seen. Now don't get me wrong, Desmond is not a bad person, he just doesn't fully live out his message. This dissonance in message and reality then creates dissonance in how people accept the message. To communicate powerfully, what you say from your mouth must be authentic - matched by the actions that you then take. So, if you are going to talk about team work, then it is important to be part of a team, spending time with them, listening, accepting others' views, collaborating. If you are going to talk about commitment, then it is important to be turning up on time, working alongside others, seeing and taking responsibility for things that are not your mistakes. If you are going to be talking about shared vision it is important to give opportunity for people to contribute ideas and discuss them and actually listen to them.

Think of great leaders, truly great ones. None of them were perfect, but what you do see is that what they communicated, what they tried to draw out from others, was in complete synchronicity with what they called out of themselves and lived. Martin Luther King called others to live out the dream that he had and that he acted.

Malala Yousafzai, when she blogged and spoke of the importance of girls' education across the world, lived out that same calling with immense bravery. For the everyday leader the same applies. Communication without authenticity is powerless.

ABCDE of communication

As a leader, effective communication is key. Remember, Howard Gardner explains leadership as "the ability to tell a story that affects the thoughts, feelings and actions of others." Therefore, in order to tell a story, you need to be able to communicate. Communication is an art, one that needs to be practised and exercised to develop it well. Now, you could write a whole book just on the topic; in fact thousands of them have been written. But this book is about the everyday basics that help you to become extraordinary, so how about 5 key things to master communication as a leader:

- **Authenticity**
- **Belief**
- **Craft** your message
- **Deliver** your message
- **Engage** the listener

We have looked at authenticity above, so let's take a look at the others.

Belief

In chapter 5, I spoke of the consultant in the hospital who entered the ward with calm assurance. That assurance that exudes from a person comes from years of experience and from the person weighing up their experience and learning from it, enabling them to face any situation with confidence.

Underpinning all of that, though, is the clarity of purpose in which they operate. They are clear on their purpose and the purpose of their mission. They know their 'why'.

Simon Sinek's TED talk on 'How great leaders inspire action' has over 39 million views. At the centre of his TED thesis is how important it is for the leader to know 'why' they are doing something and how they use this to engage followers. His book 'Start with Why'[xvi] has sold millions and highlights how your 'why' makes the 'how' and 'what' engaging and impactful. Michael Junior, American comedian, in his YouTube videos on his show piece called 'showtime', teaches how the 'why' can bring passion. He takes a singer who is in the audience and asks him to sing a song. He then explains a situation, a funeral of an uncle, and the singing took on a whole new meaning and he sang with passion and fervour. As a comedian, he then delivers the punchline. He says, "When you know your 'why' . . . your 'what' has more impact, because you are walking in or towards your purpose."

It was November 2014, and Dave Courteen and his wife Miranda organised the *'Another bite of The Last Chocolate Brownie'* ball. In 2012 they had organised the *'Last Chocolate Brownie Ball'* and had raised £10,000 for Breakthrough Breast Cancer and Woolverstone Wish charities. 2014 was time for another ball. Now if you have ever organised a ball, or a big event like it, you will know that it is fraught with challenges and hard work. But yet only two years later, Dave and Miranda were back doing another one. Why? When you had done one, why do another? Well for Dave and Miranda they had set themselves a challenge.

In 2010 Miranda had been diagnosed with a rare form of breast cancer. As she told friends of her news, someone, with reference to the line from the film Notting Hill, said, "Well you've won the last chocolate brownie this week." Miranda went through intense chemotherapy, double mastectomy and reconstructive surgery.

Dave blogged about the experience to help Miranda, himself and friends process it and this formed the content of the book, entitled 'The Last Chocolate Brownie', that was written to help readers and raise money for breast cancer charities. So why organise this second ball? Dave and Miranda will tell you that they thank God for the medical care that Miranda received and for the all clear that she has now been given. They thank God for the time with their children and the joy of seeing them travel through stages of life together. They are thankful and wanted to raise money for others to receive that same medical care. Every communication had their 'why' clearly running through it. Their aim, through book sales and the charity balls, was to raise £20,000. To date £21,500 has been raised. *"When you know your 'why'. . . your 'what' has more impact, because you are walking in or towards your purpose."*

And so, as I went to sit down at the table at the *'Another bite of The Last Chocolate Brownie'* ball, Dave introduced me to two other guests at the table: "Let me introduce you to Nick and Annette Hulme." Nick was the CEO at Ipswich hospital and Annette was his wife. I was struck instantly with the presence of these two people. Nick had presence, a calmness, a respect, an authority not demanded, but nevertheless there. He sought not to bring attention to himself but chose to greet with friendliness, with warmth and to find out about those at the table. Annette had grace and poise, worthy of royalty. Her calm, caring approach was matched by her willingness later in the evening to help in any way she could, not wishing to have any focus on herself, but just to help. They were possibly on paper the most important people at the ball. But yet every action was to support the cause and do so in a way that bought honour to others.

And so, fast forward to July 2018. This time, Nick Hulme was on the television. Not, as he often is, as the CEO of the Ipswich hospital explaining a latest success of the hospital or responding to a news report about the hospital. This time he was there as husband of Annette.

"My wife, Annette, made me promise that when I retired we would do the Coast to Coast walk together. Sadly, she died from breast cancer in January this year. A couple of weeks before she died she made me promise that I would complete the Coast to Coast in her memory and raise some money for the Breast Unit at Ipswich Hospital and St Elizabeth Hospice, whose teams cared for her during her illness. So from 18th June to 1st July this year (2018) I will be walking the 191 miles of the Coast to Coast path, with some friends and family who will be joining me for part of the way. Please give generously in memory of an extraordinary person who is loved and missed and was an inspiration to so many."

You could not help but be moved by the news report, by Nick's love for Annette and even more so when you had met them both. Nick's 'why' was clear as he spoke. *"When you know your 'why' . . . your 'what' has more impact, because you are walking in or towards your purpose."*

If you know why you are doing something it gives you the purpose and the power to stick to it, even when things are hard work. So, when you know the purpose, you can communicate this to others. The deeper and richer the purpose for the person, the richer the engagement, passion and determination for the cause. Dave, Miranda, Nick and Annette all had a deep passion for the purpose. It was therefore easy for them to communicate that in the stories they told and in the actions that they took. If you are challenged on the issue you are communicating, clarity of purpose gives you a solid rock to hold on to – a reference point.

In terms of leading, communicating purpose is crucial for engagement. Here are a couple of key pointers to help:

Venn Diagram

People have different passions and interests. So, when communicating with others, try to put the message and the reason why we you want them to engage with the issue in terms of things that engage them. Imagine a Venn diagram, circles intersecting. When communicating, try to speak into that intersection, the point where their 'why' meets your 'why'. For example, if you have a colleague that loves order and tidiness, include that in your reason. If you have a colleague that loves hitting targets, then include that in your reason. If you have a colleague that has a heart and passion for the greater good, then include that in your reason.

Passion

Think about why you have got involved in activities. Chances are it is for one of 3 reasons: 1) it interested you; 2) you had a friend who was doing it; 3) someone was talking about it passionately. As human beings, we are naturally attracted to passion and enthusiasm. Think about something you are not particularly interested in; what gets you to buy in is someone that you like talking enthusiastically about how much fun it will be. If you want work colleagues to be involved, think about the good aspects of it and talk passionately about it.

One of the things my wife and I are passionate about is the children's charity we established. It is a faith-based charity that runs holidays for children of all backgrounds. For some of the children it is their first holiday ever. For all of them, it is a place of acceptance, inclusion and fun. It is run completely by volunteers and as you look at the team over the years, it is full of people that we have just had conversations with about the work. We talked passionately about the impact it had on children, on their confidence and on their value.

We talked passionately about a group of adults who make it happen and the sense of inclusive community that they create each holiday. And quite often at the end of that conversation follows a response from them. For many, it is "How can I be involved?" For others, it is "How can I pay for a child to attend?" When you talk enthusiastically about a passion, people become impassioned.

Create a crowd

If you ever go to Covent Garden or somewhere similar, you will see street performers plying their trade. What causes you to stop and watch? Sometimes it will be because the entertainer is very good and catches your eye. Another attraction to stop and watch is if there is already a crowd there. If you have an important message to convey, particularly if it involves change, then try to create your crowd. By this I mean choose some handpicked people to test out the new approach. Then, review how it went and iron out with them any problems. You then create a fanbase, a crowd who are for the idea as they have been part of shaping it.

This was a technique I often used when starting a new initiative in my school. People like to be involved in a little challenge or investigation. So if I needed to run a new approach to teaching writing for example, I would ask a year group to test it out. The three class teachers would try it and I would ask them to present their findings. Some might be positive towards it, some a little concerned about change or workload. Both were great to involve in it, as when we asked for feedback the slightly sceptical ones would be happy to talk about their worries and how some of these did not materialise.

Change with benefits

If you are communicating some change, then thinking around change management is crucial. One of the key aspects in this is how you talk about the past. If you talk brutally about the practice that has been followed for the last 20 years, rubbishing it, then you are setting yourself up for creating a lot of enemies. It is crucial to respect the 'why' of the past, to respect the practice that worked well then and respect what is still positive now. Then explain the changes needed, in terms of building on the tried and tested purpose and practice to make the situation even better and to meet the current issues.

Story

Stories are not just for children. Story has immense power and connection and is a vital tool for connecting people to the purpose of what you are communicating. Scientists have done studies on the brains of the story teller and the story listener and what they have discovered is amazing. Story-telling activates a part of the brain that enables the listener to turn the story into their own. It causes mirroring in the brain of the story teller and listener. It releases dopamine when it experiences an emotionally charged event. Psychologists suggest that this can help the listener remember details up to 22 times more than just facts alone.[xvii] So when communicating the purpose, use story to connect the listener.

Rae looked the 60 business leaders in front of her and began to speak. "Let me tell you about James. I first met James when I sat next to him in the Leadership for Life training. I could see that James had amazing potential but James could not see that in himself."

Rae was the leader of the Together Project at The Mix youth provision in Stowmarket. This project was established to help young people like James who needed a fresh start and needed practical help and the Together Project was about working with local business to provide training and opportunities to help them.
So, Rae continued the story: "James was a young man who had struggled with drug addiction. After the Leadership for Life course, James got himself a job, but this had not lasted long. James was still up for the fresh start – however, he needed help. So I got in contact with some of you in the room about James and giving him an opportunity. One of you gave him that opportunity, and helped him with training. The offer of longer-term work was there if he could go self-employed. So again, I contacted one of you who worked in advice in this area and you helped him set this up and explained it to him. As a result, James is now working, doing well and loving his new start. He wants you to know, if it was not for the Leadership for Life course and the support of The Mix and the Together Project, he would be dead by now. Instead, he is enjoying his new start. I want to say thank you to you for your support of people like James."

James' story is powerful. It is a story of transformation. It is a story of local involvement. It is a story where people understand how their involvement can make a difference. It is a story that creates a draw, encouraging people to follow the same example. Where it becomes powerful communication is when it is a story told by someone who passionately believes in the story they were telling. Rae knows James. Rae knows first-hand the impact of community and business involvement in the Together Project. There is no cognitive dissonance here, as the story and storyteller are rooted in integrity and practice, told with passion and from the heart.

Emotional connection

In communication, facts and figures are important, but what gets people to connect to the purpose at the core of your message is when you connect to people's emotions. Why did we get involved in helping Dave and Miranda in their charity ball? Because of the emotional connection. We had travelled with them in their journey. So, when they asked for help in selling tickets and setting up, the response was 'yes' because we could see the difference the money raised would make for others who found themselves in that same situation. So, when communicating, explain the difference it will make to the staff, the customers, those your mission serves. The difference it makes to lives. The social, emotional and physical benefits.

Craft your message

Powerful communication as a leader does not normally happen by accident. Often messages are crafted over time, as the leader speaks, refines, speaks, refines. This refinement is crucial for an ongoing message, trying to engage and maintain engagement. There are also some key things for every message that will help delivery.

Be clear to get others clear

Make sure that you are really clear yourself on what you want to communicate. What is the purpose? What are you hoping to achieve?

Consider aids & barriers

When you communicate, try to consider what might be stopping the message landing. Are there things the person has experienced that might hinder the message? What is the environment like? What has happened that day that might affect it? Take this situation for example.

It had been a long hard day for Jane. Her class of 30 eight-year-olds had been quite challenging that day. The day had ended with an angry parent at the classroom door, which had taken a lot of time and energy to help her understand what had actually happened with her child that day. She sat in her room with her head in her hands, somewhat exhausted, when there was a knock at the door and in walked Simon, a young enthusiastic deputy head, to talk to her about a new approach to reading with the children.

Now it doesn't take a rocket scientist to work out how effective this conversation might be at this point. 24 hours later might be better!

It is also worth considering who might be the best person to convey the message. For example, if there is any history that needs to be accounted for. In this story, Jane used to be Simon's mentor, guiding and advising him when he was a newly qualified teacher. In a recent interview for the deputy headteacher position, Simon and Jane were both interviewed and Simon was appointed, much to Jane's annoyance. The situation is still a little sore for Jane. In this case, sending Simon to deliver the message is not the greatest decision in the first place.

Words, tone and body language

Communication is not just about words. In fact, only 7% of what we communicate is from the words. 38% of it is in the tone we use and 55% is in the body language we use. The simple words, "I would like to talk to you about your work," can convey completely different communication with different tone and body language.

Say it with a smile and warm tone and the person will readily chat to you about it, expecting praise and value. Say it with arms folded and a short curt tone and the head of the listener will drop as they know they are in for another telling off. A difficult message in words can be conveyed with more effect by balancing a caring, respectful tone and body language. Going into a meeting to talk about an initiative that you hope to roll out also needs the right tone. Too bullish and you are likely to get a reaction. Enter with a nervous body language and unsure tone and 'the workplace tiger is sure to run rings round you and give you a mauling..

Craft your words

Words can be emotive. So when talking to someone, think about the words you use and the different perspectives that people can take from a word. Take the phrase, "I disagree." For someone who has had a lot of criticism, that will evoke a stronger reaction. Rewording things can show understanding. For example: *"I recognise the benefits of what you are proposing. I wonder if we could examine another way of looking at this."*

You can still talk about your same point but by starting with a recognition of their point of view and presenting it as something to explore, you are less likely to get an emotional reaction and thus lose the potential to engage them.

Five Prompts

Steve Adams, in his book 'The Centre Brain', talks about 5 Prompts for Persuasive Power[xviii]. It explains 5 key things that great communicators and advertisers use to enhance the power of their words. Look at how this can help engage staff to look after customers:

Idea Rather than tell someone to do something, present it as an idea. This gets engagement from the listener and involvement as they are being invited in. Rather than tell the staff member you need to use a set phrase to greet people coming into reception, put it as an idea.*"I would like visitors to feel like part of the family to increase our return rate. I wonder if we could test a new approach with customers when we greet them ."*

Why Explaining why makes the what and how sound more interesting. In the sentence above, it has the 'why'. We want engagement from the customer, we want them to feel like family, we want them to return.

Contrast Try to present a contrast with what you are hoping for. *Eg, If we take the option I am presenting then this could be the outcome. If we don't, then this will be the outcome.* So with the initiative to change the approach with customers above, giving the difference it will make: *"Our return rate of customers is low at the moment. If we continue to start by asking what are they here for today with no welcome, they will feel that it is clinical and less personal and so won't want to return."*

Pictorialise	Create a picture in people's mind. Tell a story, present the information in a way people can see it in their mind's eye. "Imagine customers feeling happier when they walk in our door, knowing this is a place they are looked after. Imagine sales increasing and positive social media comments on our social media platforms."
Emotional	Speaking to the inner emotional brain develops warmth and engagement, *eg*, talking about happier customers, talking about the difference it can make to the listener: *"We want every customer to feel valued and like you would want a family member to feel when they come into our company. Imagine, for example, how your granny would want to be treated. Imagine her feeling valued and cared for."*

Deliver your message

Now, if you have an important message, something that needs to happen, you could call a meeting. Stand up in front of everyone and tell them. Give them a torrent of information, a well-prepared PowerPoint, a story, and send them on their way, safe in the knowledge that you have told them what needs to be done. There is nothing wrong with this. But there is an even greater way to ensure that the message gets across.

One-off deliveries of important messages have their place, but they are like filling a bath with a torrent of water. Sure, at that moment the bath is full of nice warm water. But after a while the water turns cold, the plug leaks a little. Within a week the bath is cold and half full. Within two weeks there is just a puddle at the bottom and the water is losing its clarity.

Within three there is just a scum mark where the water once stood. A far better way is to 'fill the bath by the dripping tap'. Give an initial fill, but keep ensuring that the message is being drip, drip, drip, drip fed at every opportunity, keeping the water warm and topped up.

Hannah Isher, who I worked with in the early 2000s, was an expert at the art of 'filling the bath by the dripping tap'. You see Hannah was not a lover of standing in front of large crowds telling them what to do. Hannah was Early Years leader in the school I led as headteacher. She took on an Early Years department that lacked a clarity of purpose; it had a range of expertise on the team but it needed to work with one accord. Hannah's expertise was living the vision that she had. She modelled it to staff in the way she dealt with children, she talked constantly about what she was doing, why she was doing it and how it helped. I term this approach creating 'Miranda Moments'. If you watch the TV programme, 'Miranda', you will see the technique that Miranda, the star of the show, uses. At points in the show, she turns to the camera and explains her thoughts to the audience. This technique brings a deeper understanding of the comedy and helps the audience to bond with her.

Hannah used this approach too. She would turn to those around her and explain what was going on. These 'Miranda moments' ensured that her staff could see, hear and understand what the vision was. When she saw good practice she would praise it, drawing attention to the staff member that had demonstrated it. When we praise those who are 'executing the message' we draw attention to it; the behaviour modelled is seen as something that will draw praise. And so, those you are addressing seek to also model that same behaviour. As a consequence, the message is alive and being passed from person to person. 'Miranda moments' are simple and easy to create. They require little planning and like the 'dripping tap keeps the bath full', they keep the message ongoing.

Helping your team to see communication as an ongoing journey is crucial. One of the key ways of doing this is being prepared to 'Spot, Speak and Synergise' the message you want them to keep live. Lauren, my former deputy head, is an absolute guru when it comes to English teaching and assessment principles. Lauren could explain clearly to staff the approach required, but what set Lauren apart was her rigour in follow up. When she saw good practice she would praise it, reminding staff why it was important. When the practice was not quite right, she would remind staff what we were aiming for and why we needed to do it. When you spot it being done well, speak about it and synergise or remind people of the initial communication you gave on this. When you spot it not done so well, challenge it in a way to develop people positively and synergise it back to the initial communication.

Engage the Listener

At the risk of alienating half of my readers that have got this far in the book, I have to confess that I used to own a towing caravan. One of the things that I learnt early on was how to reverse the car towards the tow hitch and align it as close as possible so that it was easy to lower the van onto the tow bar on the car. I often would reverse the car with the boot open and rear seats down so that I could see where the tow hitch was. I learnt that it was far easier to move the car to where the hitch was, than have to pull 1 tonne of caravan towards the car by hand.

This is a simple metaphor for an important aspect of communication. Before you do any talking to anyone, the best way to ensure your communication brings people with you is to:

- Know where your listener is
- Find points of connection
- Start from that point of connection

- Gently ease them from the connection point to where you want to take them

This is about an effective use of your communication energy. It ensures that there is as little a gap as possible between you and the listener that might lose them. The key to this is effective listening. This is listening for understanding, not superficial listening to make them think their view is important or so you can then finally get on with your important topic.

Speaking last allows you to understand the person and enables you to speak with targeted wisdom. Listening for understanding, and then targeting what you say, is like the difference between firing random arrows up in the air and aiming one arrow right at the gold centre of the target. It is a much more efficient use of arrows!

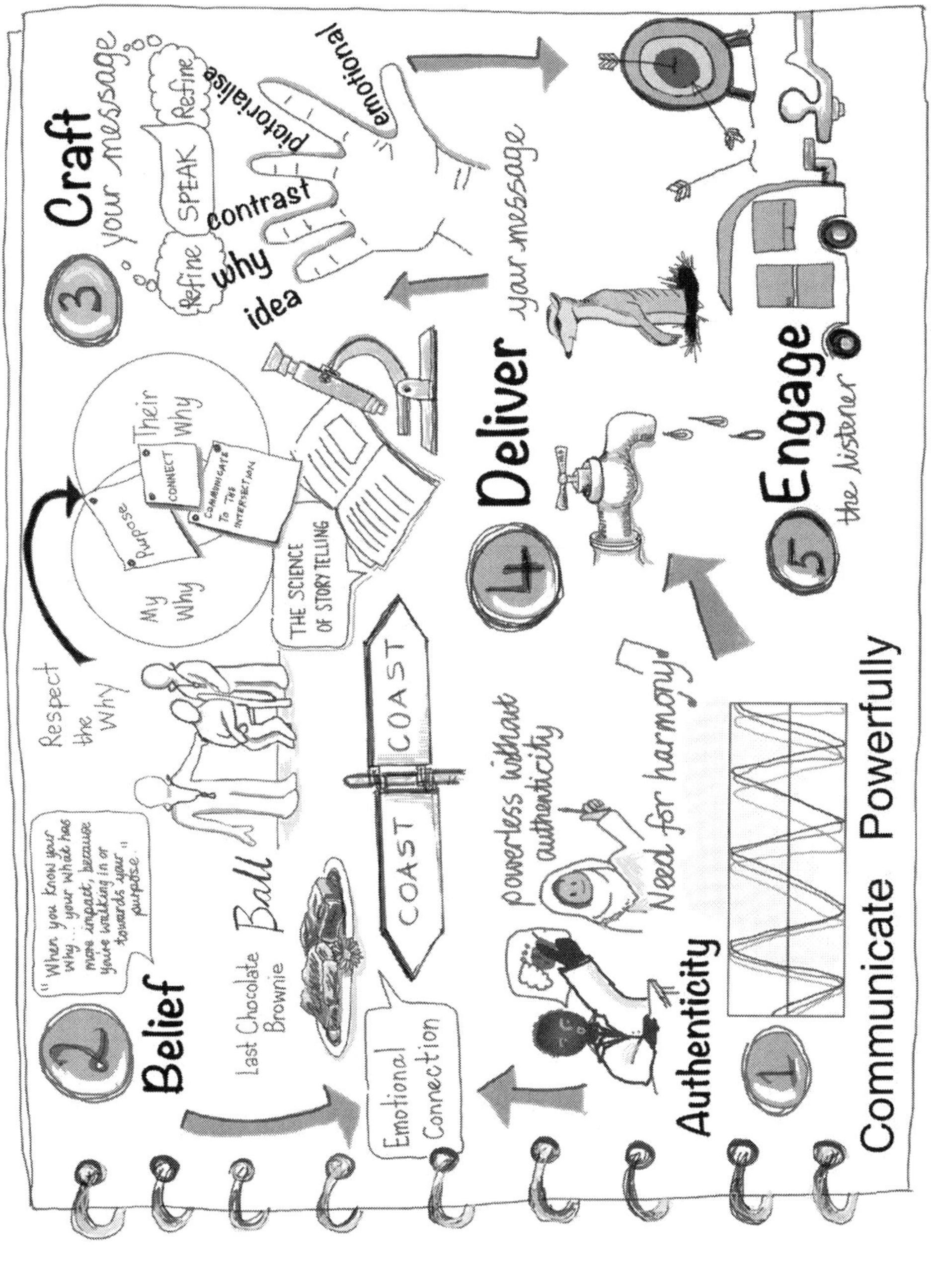
Communicate Powerfully
1 Authenticity
powerless without authenticity
Need for harmony!
2 Belief
"When you know your why... your what has more impact, because you're walking in or towards your purpose."
Last Chocolate Brownie
Ball
Emotional Connection
COAST
COAST
COAST
Respect the Why
My Why
Purpose
CONNECT
COMMUNICATE TO THE INTERSECTION
Their Why
THE SCIENCE OF STORY TELLING
3 Craft your message
Refine
SPEAK
Refine
why
idea
contrast
pictorialise
emotional
4 Deliver your message
5 Engage the listener

Personal Reflection – Communicate

Authenticity

Are there any areas of communication dissonance where your actions don't match your words?

Belief

What are you passionate about? Is that the core of what you communicate?

Craft your message

Consider something you plan to communicate. Consider each element below.

Element	Key Question	Thoughts
Clarity	*Am I clear? What is the key point I am making?*	
Aids & barriers	*What barriers might stop this message landing? Person, environment, time of day?*	
Words, tone & body language	*What is important about my tone and body language to give power to the message?*	
Craft your words	*Which key words should I start with that evoke the right emotion?*	

Personal Reflection – Communicate

Deliver your message		
Consider something you plan to communicate, using these elements from the chapter.		
Element	Key Question	Thoughts
Create a Crowd	*Who can create a crowd with me?*	
Change with benefits	*What are the benefits of the change?*	
Story	*What stories of impact or metaphorical stories can I tell?*	
Emotional connection	*What difference will this make to people's lives?*	

Engage
What are my points of connection with the audience?

Chapter 7: Develop Expertise

Simon, Steve, Brian and Lauren

"Expertise comes when the knowledge and experience gained is processed for understanding. Authority in this area comes when the core learning is distilled to its pure essence and generates core thinking that is dextrous, applicable in different contexts. When this is conveyed thoughtfully to help others improve, you are seen as having technical expertise and authority in this area."

I guess, when you really know your stuff, it would be easy to get big headed. When you are an authority in an area it would be easy to walk into a room and command it and laud it over the people present. But when you meet a true expert, they don't behave like that.

Simon was one of those true experts. So assured of who he was as a person and as an expert, he did not need to laud it over others. Instead he walked into the room with calmness and respectful humility. "Hello, I'm Simon Timson. Nice to meet you." Simon didn't know I was the other speaker who was on stage after him as he shook my hand. I was just somebody in the room. Simon then took to the front of a group of business leaders in Shrewsbury and started to talk passionately about his work.

Simon is the Performance Director of the Lawn Tennis Association (LTA). He took up the role in 2016 following the Olympic Games in Rio, where he fulfilled his final duties as the Performance Director of UK Sport. Prior to his role at UK Sport, Simon spent two years with the England and Wales Cricket Board, firstly as Head of Science & Medicine, followed by the role of Head of the England Development Programme. Simon was also Skeleton Performance Director of the British Bobsleigh & Skeleton Association from 2000 to 2006. Simon's CV was rich with experiences and success. His aim as UK Sport Performance Director was to help the UK get more medals in the 'post host' Olympic games, something they achieved. He now had his eyes on developing British tennis from grass roots up.

Simon commanded the room that day. He spoke with authority and expertise. And yet within the room there were business leaders from all sorts of industry and commerce. Simon could not be an expert in all of those areas. And yet, he had authority in the room. People wanted to hear what they could learn about improving performance.

As I took to the stage next, a son of a farmhand and a former headteacher, the little dark voices in my head told me that this was going to go horribly wrong. They had heard the expert in Simon - what would business leaders want to know from a mere ex-headteacher whose CV was nowhere near as impressive? And yet, they did listen and some asked for my business card afterwards. They listened because I spoke to them about what it takes to lead a high-performing team. They listened because my experience in leading large teams of people and the quality top tips were helpful to them.

Simon may not have known the intricacies of each and every one of their businesses but he knew about how to create high performance in an organisation. He's an expert in it. I, too, may not have known the intricacies of each of their businesses but I knew about how to work with teams and what leadership qualities and strategies developed high performance in a team.

As leaders in our respective fields, we had a perspective that was helpful to the business leaders in the room. But neither of us had the 'technical or professional expertise' in each of their businesses. So, can you be a leader without technical or professional expertise in that area? Can you successfully lead improvement and development in an area you are not an expert in? Many have, so what are the key ingredients for success? What do you need to bring to situations like this?

On Twitter recently someone posted the question, "Can you be a good school leader without having been a good teacher?" It's a great question. I know a number of brilliant teachers, who have struggled to lead others. I equally can name a few headteachers who are not great teachers, but who lead their school very well. But, of course, the very best headteachers can teach well and lead their school well because they are clear on what makes good quality education and can teach it to others.

Can you be a leader in industry without being an expert in that sector? The same thinking can be applied to business. Can you lead well in business if you are not an expert in the field your business is in? Can a CEO of a chocolate company lead well if he is not a chocolatier? My father-in-law, Brian, was a trained carpenter and surveyor and then spent many years as a manager in the building preservation industry. His last fifteen years of work, though, were as a manager in a plastics factory. Plastic is a very different medium to work with compared to wood. And yet, he had credibility with the workers. He had credibility in the field of management, he listened to his employees to understand the plastics business and was prepared to learn fast in the area of plastics.

If Brian the carpenter can lead in a plastics factory, then there is the possibility of leading without full technical expertise. But, what Brian had was:

- a professional expertise of business and managing others
- principles that he adapted from his technical knowledge of carpentry
- a humility and willingness to learn a new field fast

Those are three core principles to take with you in any leadership arena, especially where you may not have a technical understanding of the product that you work in.

- Bring the expertise that you do have *eg*, leadership, marketing or sales.
- Adapt principles that you have experience of from other arenas.
- Be humble. Look, listen and learn from others who have that expertise.

How technical expertise helps

Of course, professional or technical expertise in an area is helpful. Used well, it enables your leadership to reach a higher level as it can give you credibility. Credibility as a leader comes when you are authentic with those that you serve. You are reliable and deliver what you promise. You develop intimate relationships with those that you lead and your approach in leadership is to serve others. But credibility also comes from your knowledge and experience of the field that you work in and how you share that knowledge with those who are under your leadership. Your technical expertise shapes your leadership.

Understanding the issues

If your team know that you have worked your way up and have technical expertise in your industry, they will have a sense that you understand the challenges that they face. You will explain the next steps forward as a company, relating to the work that they do. When the latest health and safety change enters your industry, you will lead the changes with an understanding of how it impacts on those working 'on the shop floor'. The technical expertise gives an insight that fuels leadership. It also stops anyone 'pulling the wool over your eyes' as they try to misrepresent things to get their own way. Your technical expertise allows you to know what is correct and what isn't.

Developing staff

The role of a leader includes developing staff to be the best they can be. When you ask staff to work to higher standards, you do so with a knowledge of what can be achieved as you have done it.

When they question what that looks like in practice, a leader with technical or professional expertise is able to give them clarity.

Clarity of vision

My role as a consultant often involves visiting schools to help the leadership understand an issue more clearly. Having spent 30 years in education, 17 of which as a headteacher, it is my field of expertise. I know how a school should tick. As I walk around a school I can see what is on the surface but my experience means that I know what sorts of things can contribute to that. One school I visited was ok. Nothing was particularly bad in children's behaviour but there was a lack of respect. Wall displays were pleasant enough but lacked purpose. Staff were friendly enough but lacked confidence. Peeling back the layers, I could see that at the core was a lack of vision for the best for children from the leadership and therefore from staff. There was no sense of urgency, importance or rigour, and that meant just about ok was ok. It was heading in one direction. I could spot this because I was a teacher and because I am a leader in education. Technical expertise helps you focus the vision as you know what high quality in your field looks like. You know the layers of purpose, values, vision, mission that sit beneath the day-to-day policies and actions.

Expertise that brings reassurance

"It's impossible," said the worried teacher. "These pupils are so far behind, we will never get them to where they need to be." There was despair in her words and her tone. She was not a bad teacher. She worked incredibly hard and wanted the very best for the children. But, to meet the targets set just felt overwhelming.

As she finished speaking, all eyes turned to the other side of the room where the deputy head sat, chairing the pupil progress meeting. A sense of calm oozed from her and time at that point seemed to stand still. You see, Lauren the deputy head, had taught for a number of years in different contexts. She had gained quality knowledge of pedagogy, how to teach reading, writing and maths and had refined the core essence that could, like a consultant's medicine, be applied here. "If we keep doing the same things, we will get the same result. We need a different approach here," she reassured the group. She then explained a new approach, that was based on a rich analysis of the children's current position. By looking at those that were below expectation in one area and targeting the one weaker area, it focused intervention time and energy better. She then modelled this to them and spent time over the next two weeks working alongside them to plan interventions to boost the children's performance. Her technical expertise, modelling and mentoring them in it, enabled the teachers to improve their skills and knowledge and improve the children's learning.

But in all reality, the leader in a company is unlikely to be an expert in absolutely every area of the company. A headteacher of a school is unlikely to be an expert in every single area of the curriculum, behaviour management and special educational needs. Now, in an ideal world, the leader would have a breadth of experience in their company, charity or school. A breadth really helps your leadership, you understand the issues and someone cannot pull the technical wool over your eyes. A breadth helps you formulate the vision and direction and explain it to people at all levels in your organisation.

So, whether you are an expert or not, there are some key things to learn about expertise.

Stages of expertise

Steve Jackman, a good friend of mine, is a business leader. He has worked for large multi-national companies (Britvic, Diageo and a subsidiary of print firm Konica Minolta). His expertise is in purchasing and marketing. He has years of experience in it. When he first started at the Konica Minolta subsidiary, he was brought in for his purchasing and marketing expertise. He had developed this expertise over many years because he had used methods and strategies in different contexts. He had been able to refine it down to the pure essence of what worked in purchasing and marketing in different contexts. So, when he started at this print company he knew what core essence was needed. The impact in his time there saw an increase in revenue from £1 million to £8 million in his department.

His role was leading in this area, but he recognised that in order to perform this role effectively he needed to learn about the print industry. I asked him whether anyone questioned his validity when he started there as he was not from the print industry? Most recognised the experience he brought, but he remembered one person in particular who was unsure of his credentials. Steve's approach was to focus his energy on those who engaged with him and demonstrate his impact. His impact then demonstrated his credentials.

To gain expertise in a field, you need to travel through 5 stages: knowledge, experience, reason, conviction and respect.

Knowledge	Experience	Reason	Conviction	Respect
What do you know?	What experiences generated this?	Have you weighed it and measured it and know how to apply it?	Have you applied it in different contexts, and therefore convey it with confidence?	Can you convey it with thoughtfulness and compassion to help others?

Expertise comes when the knowledge and experience gained is processed for understanding. Authority in this area comes when the core learning is distilled to its pure essence and generates core thinking that is dextrous, applicable in different contexts. When this is conveyed thoughtfully to help others improve, you are seen as having technical expertise and authority in this area. So when you share an idea with someone and they question how the thinking can be applied in a different context, the question does not throw you as you know your knowledge and experience has been reasoned and refined to suit the new need. The courage of your conviction comes because you have been able to refine your knowledge and experience in a range of contexts to discover the very essence that can be applied in many contexts.

What if you are in a new field?

James carefully placed his briefcase down on his desk. He looked back through the internal office window to see his new work colleagues watching him from their desks. It was his first morning as their new boss and he was going to speak to them in ten minutes in the first of his new morning briefings. He opened the briefcase locks to hear that satisfying click, click as he lifted the lid. Beneath his cellophaned sandwiches were a few papers, including his agenda for his briefing meeting with staff. He carefully lifted it out and placed it on his desk. Imposter syndrome washed over him as he looked down at the letterhead for Confident Clothing. He had no training in clothing retail. All of his experience, 15 years' worth, was in the paint industry. He had been brought in as customer services director as the company was struggling to maintain its customers and therefore revenue and the CEO was desperate to turn the tide. How he approached it with his customer services team was crucial.

70% of leaders are reported to experience Imposter syndrome. It is therefore is no surprise that when we are operating out of our comfort zone or in the case of James above, outside of our expertise, we can feel unsure of ourselves. So how can you lead yourself in this context?

Firstly, we need to recognise what we do bring to the role. We may not be an expert in all areas, but what do we bring?

Know your end goal

As in any area of leadership, the key is knowing where you are taking people. What is the core direction the organisation needs to head in? What is its purpose?

Chances are that if you are in a position where you are not an expert, you have been brought in for a particular reason. If, like James, it is because of an area of company weakness that needs improving, you need to be clear about what 'good' looks like in that area, so that you can make it clear to staff.

Know what you know

If, like James, you do not have direct technical experience of the new company's field, what technical expertise do you have? As a leader, you will have an experience of working with people. What have you distilled that you can use in this context? James, in our story above, was not an expert in clothing. But he had fifteen years' worth of customer service expertise. He didn't know how to create the perfect outfit, but he did know what good customer service looked like. He knew what good support systems looked like. He knew what good phone manner looked like. All of which his new company needed a lot of movement on, based on his previous visits before starting.

Know what you don't know

Nothing is more annoying to people than others masquerading as experts in a field they are not. Do not be tempted to pretend. People sniff out fakes quickly and it will do damage to credibility that you might have in other areas. James had his sentence all worked out if he faced something he was unsure of. "Tell me a little about how that works for you here at Confident Clothing. Customer service is my area of expertise and because I worked with a different product I would like to see how my experience can help in this context."

Listen and learn fast

If you are a new leader, the employees will be nervous about you. They may have heard rumours and are not sure if they will feel safe. In my first permanent post as a headteacher, it was to amalgamate two schools to become one school. There was a rumour going around the office that I was planning to bring in all my own office staff. I've no idea where it came from and I quickly quashed it and reassured people. One way that you can quickly build respect from your team is to spend time listening. James's sentence above starts with that: "Tell me a little about how that works here for you." By asking questions, it allows you to learn about the business, understand the issues and glean areas for improvement. This allows you to learn. Learning fast is important, as it helps you build credibility.

Build a team around you to complement your skills

Imagine you are a football coach. You spent years playing as a centre forward putting the goals away. Now you are a football coach.

You have a general knowledge of the game and your speciality is developing the strikers. But when it comes to defence, it is not your expertise. So, when you look to bring in other coaching staff, you want a goalkeeping coach and you want a coach who can help develop your defenders and midfield if you can. The same applies to business, education and third sector leadership. Look to develop a trustworthy team that complements your experience of the industry and your style of leadership. As a headteacher, I knew my curricular strengths of Maths, RE, PE. I knew my expertise in developing people. So, when looking for a new deputy or assistant head I looked for expertise in areas like SEND (Special Educational Needs and Disability) or English or Assessment.

If you are an expert

You could be forgiven for thinking that if you are an expert in your field, that you have got it made as a leader. However, like any skill or experience that you might have, it needs to be used carefully.

Hold your sword lightly

As a leader, when you have 'been there and done that', there is a real danger of becoming a micro-manager. You have done the job and you are an expert and so you know what good quality looks like. The temptation is to then dictate exactly how it should be done. When someone doesn't meet the standards you expect, you are then quick to correct them and tell them how it should be done. This is dangerous as it disempowers the member of your team. They are afraid to make mistakes and so are quick to cover up things. It can alienate them. As an expert leader, it is important to hold our knowledge and experience sword lightly and remember the last part of the process – respect.

Convey your knowledge with thoughtfulness and compassion. A good leader lifts people up, encourages them to become better. So, even when correcting someone in an area where they have not met high standards, it should be in a way to help them aspire to be better.

Remember you're the leader

Your role as a leader is to provide vision and help people get there. The second danger of being an expert is that we get so wrapped up in the current, the day-to-day and the nitty-gritty that we lose sight of the role as a leader to provide direction and vision.

Coach your staff

Trevor Waldock, in his book 'To Plant a Walnut Tree',[xix] talks about the importance of those with wisdom and experience to act as an elder to others. He reminds readers of the importance of the village elder who acts with wisdom, seeking to coach and counsel those who are younger in their leadership and role. Coaching is one of the aspects of leadership outlined by Daniel Goleman[xx] and for me it is one of the most powerful. It places value in people as the coach has an unconditional positive regard for the team member - that they can take ownership of something and be successful. The temptation as an expert is to tell someone how to do it. By using four simple coaching questions you can instil deep learning.

G – What is your **goal?**
R – What is the **reality?** Good and bad.
O – What are your **options?**
W – Which of these options is the best one to solve the problem?

You don't know everything

When you are an expert in a field, there is a temptation to think you actually know it all. My wife regularly reminds me that I do not know it all. As a leader, surround yourself with people who will help you keep perspective.

So what about expertise?

Can you be a leader with technical expertise in your field? Most certainly and it gives you a clarity and an advantage, but make sure you keep to your role of providing vision and use your expertise wisely.

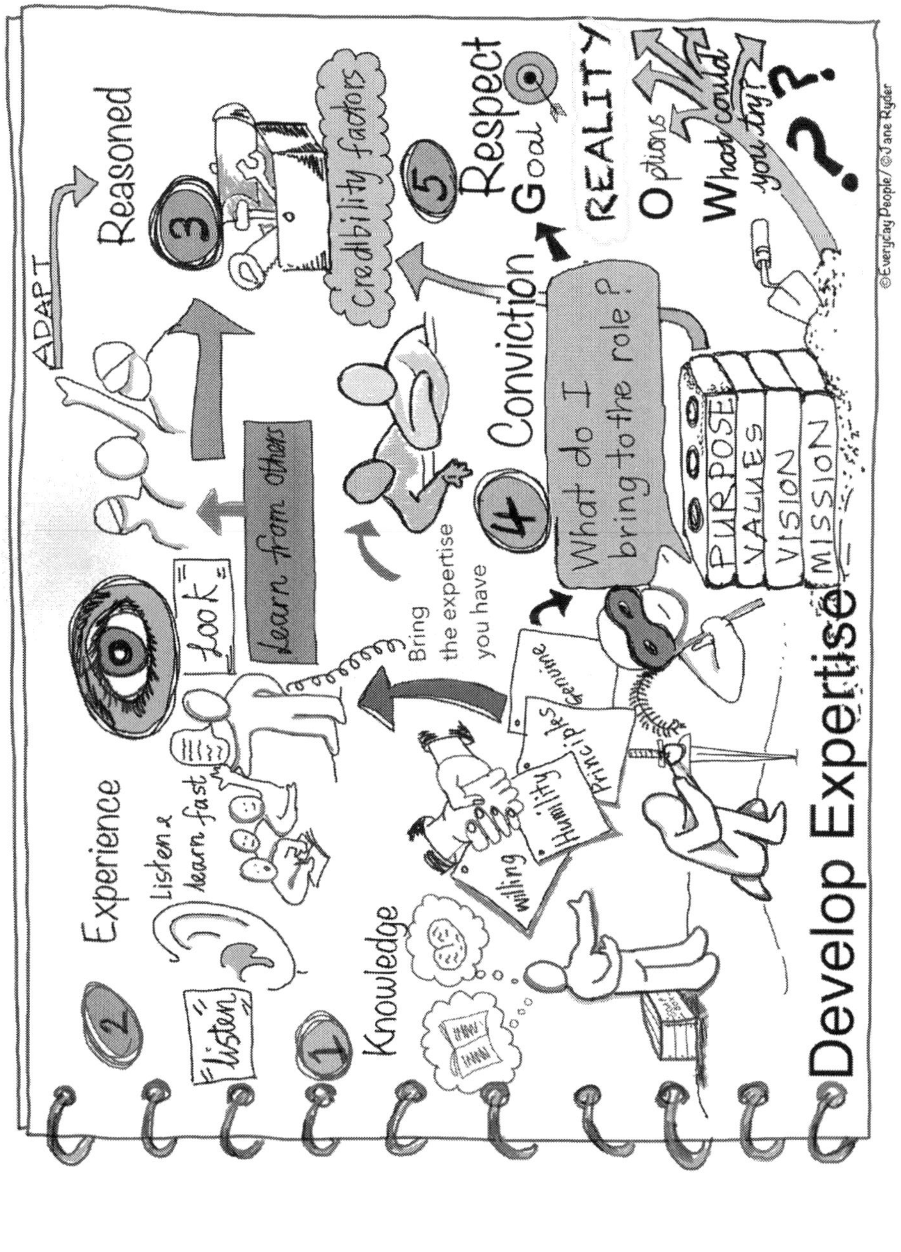
Develop Expertise
1
Knowledge
2
Experience
listen
Listen & learn fast
look
learn from others
ADAPT
3
Reasoned
credibility factors
Bring the expertise you have
willing
Humility
Principles
Genuine
4
Conviction
What do I bring to the role?
PURPOSE
VALUES
VISION
MISSION
5
Respect
Goal
REALITY
Options
What could you try?
©Everyday People/©Jane Ryder

Personal Reflection – Expertise

What is your Technical Expertise?
Knowledge *What do you know?*
Experience: *What experiences generated this?*
Reason: *What is the essence that you have weighed and measured?*
Conviction: *Have you applied this essence in different contexts?*
Respect: *Where have you conveyed it to 'lift people up'?*

Personal Reflection – Expertise

Lack Technical Expertise?
Your goal: ***What do you need to know?***
Who you are: ***What are you good at already?***
What you don't know: ***What are your gaps in knowledge and skills?***
How to learn fast: ***Who can help you learn?*** ***What training or experience will help you learn?***

Are you already the expert?
Hold sword lightly: ***What do you need to be careful with?***
Coach your staff: ***How can you ask questions to draw it out from them rather than tell them?***
What you don't know: ***What are your gaps in knowledge and skills?***

Chapter 8:

Have a Strategic Perspective

Julian and Alvin

"To think strategically starts with you, as leader, getting the purpose clear and then making it clear to everyone."

"Dad, they've closed the road and I don't know where I'm going." These were the words, but the panic in her voice emphasised the sense of emergency. Sophie, my eldest daughter, was on her way to be a leader in a youth residential and she was part of the group arriving early to set things up. She had allowed plenty of time, and knew where she was going, but was not prepared for the only route to be blocked. She needed my help. But before I helped her can you guess the first question that I asked her? Yes, you've guessed it . . . "Where are you?" Before you can help anyone who is lost, you need to know their starting point.

The same applies to developing any kind of strategic direction for a company, school, charity or organisation. In order to help someone get to where they need to be, you need clarity on where they are.

Having a strategic perspective is important whether you are starting something new or maintaining progress of your organisation. Organisations can pay companies millions for helping them write their strategy, but is it really that complicated? Can it be boiled down to something that we can all work with?

It's like a journey

Think of it like going on a journey, like going on a family holiday. Firstly, you sit down as a family and decide why you want to go on holiday. What is it you are looking for? Rest, relaxation, fun, entertainment? Then, it is where to go. Where have we been in the past? What are we looking to do? Where would we like to go? The family talk about what you already have for the journey and what you need to gather or purchase. In the old days, before satnavs and Google maps, you would then get out a map and look for the destination.

You find where you are on the map and then plot the route of how to get there. Today, even with Google maps and satnavs, it needs to know where you are, your starting point, to plot the journey. Strategic planning is on the same principle. I think strategic planning is down to these 6 simple steps:

Purpose	What is your vision for your organisation? What are the values that underpin it?
Position	Where are we now? What is working and what is not?
Proposal	What do you want something to look like? Where do you want to be?
Priority	What is your priority? What do you need to focus on to get to the destination?
Partners	Who can help you get to where you want to be and what skills do you need?
Plan	What steps are needed to get you there?

Purpose

Imagine taking part in an exercise where people are invited to walk around in a circle marked out by rope on the floor. After a minute it starts to become boring and meaningless. Losing your purpose and direction is like that – aimlessly walking around. A clear purpose drives the day-to-day, drives review of what is happening and what we need to do next.

My last school had a mission of 'promoting achievement and success'. In order to fulfil this we had 4 key elements: Inspiration, Aspiration, Collaboration, Expectation. We had an expectation for high standards, helping children aspire to do their best. We wanted the learning experience to be inspiring and collaborated with stakeholders to help the children achieve. So, when we looked at a new initiative, we asked, "Will it inspire children? Will it help us aspire to higher standards? Will people collaborate to achieve it?" In my work as a consultant now I work with schools and businesses. You might think it is simple, and in some ways it is. A school is there to teach children, a manufacturing company is there to sell what it has manufactured. But the strongest purpose is when people know why they are doing it. For example, if you are teaching children from disadvantaged backgrounds and your purpose is to give them life and career choices as an adult, then that purpose drives the choice of trips you put on, the curriculum you teach and intervention techniques to improve outcomes.

I work with a Health and Spa company called Mosaic. One of their core values is that their clubs should be friendly and fun to belong to. Therefore, their approach as you book, arrive and plan for your treatment is friendly. Any developments, new programmes or initiatives also fit that value. Another value is listening to customer opinions. So, when one of their clubs, the Shrewsbury Club, considered feedback from members about providing more for families, they had those two drivers in mind. Alvin, Centre Manager, came up with a cunning plan. What if they decided to provide free children's activities as part of an adult member's affiliation? There was a risk that this might lead to a drop of income raised by charging for children's activities already in place. But the drivers of listening to customers and being friendly drove the idea. The impact was massive. Members were delighted, told their friends and this led to a rise in sign-ups as members, raised income and a lot of very happy members and children.

In my work now, working with organisations, I still am surprised by the number of companies, schools and charities that are not clear on their purpose. Being clear and getting others clear on this is absolutely crucial if you are going to have any strategic direction. To think strategically starts with you, as leader, getting the purpose clear and then making it clear to everyone. If you can, it works best when you keep it simple and easy to remember. Have one single purpose and try to keep the values at 5 or less (or even better 3 or less) to help your team remember them.

In April 2017 I established a company Everyday Leader. Everyday Leader's purpose is to 'inspire, develop and equip everyday people to lead'. We do this through training, consultancy and coaching. We have 5 key values that drive all the work that we do:

Passion	We love what we do. We are totally committed to helping people lead.
Authenticity	Our approach is genuine and honest. We listen, understand and give practical support.
Integrity	We believe actions should be true, noble, right, pure, lovely and admirable.
Determination	We'll model leadership courage, resolve, grit and persistence.
Adaptability	We'll help you look at things objectively and develop the ability to adapt.

And, if you pushed me to three of them, I would say that we passionately develop authentic leaders of integrity. (Passion, Authenticity, Integrity.)

So, if we are asked to help an organisation, the first thing we ask ourselves is "Will it help inspire, develop or equip people to lead?" If someone enquires about joining us, we ask are they passionate about leadership and do they give off that vibe?

Are they people of integrity? Are they authentic and can they understand the situation and give clear, simple balanced advice without jargon and trivialities? Are they real? When we design training, we make sure it is passionate and engaging and fun! We make sure the advice and tips are based on rich theory but honed in real experience. Get clear on the purpose and the practice then follows.

Position

In 2005, I was asked to go into a school as a consultant headteacher and 'maintain the progress' as the current headteacher had left quickly and a new one had not been appointed. I went in a few days before officially starting to have a look around and gauge the current state of play. Within a few hours of looking through the school, office and paperwork it was apparent to me that the job I had been asked to do of 'maintain progress' was a very different one to what was needed. There was very little progress to maintain and the starting point was a very different one; the basics and the foundations needed putting in first. My report on the current state of play was in the local education authority's inbox by the following morning. Knowing your current position is a key part of strategy and if you start in the wrong position, like a building with weak foundations, you are likely to leave gaps that will cause you problems later.

The key for ensuring an effective starting point is confident celebration followed by critical consideration.

Confident celebration

In my experience, many organisations do review their position, but they fall into the trap of only finding fault in their situation. "This is a nightmare," or "It's all rubbish," are phrases that are wheeled out in this kind of review. This often means that any good is often ignored and then 'the baby is thrown out with the bathwater'.

However, when you start with Confident Celebration, it a) helps you feel better about the current position; b) creates a sense of thankfulness that reduces the stress hormone cortisol and aids creative thinking for finding solutions; c) gives you some positive pillars to build improvement on; d) ensures good parts are not thrown out. Ignore this part at your peril.

Confident celebration then needs to go hand in hand with critical consideration to get real clarity.

Critical consideration

When you know what is working well and the areas to improve, then it helps you invest energy on the right things. Critical Consideration – an open, honest reflection and review – is then crucial to get a clear picture. In order to go forward, you need to look back and know where you are building from.

The Japanese have a word 'hansei' which describes process of an honest assessment of problem areas, focusing on what went wrong and on creating clear plans for ensuring that it does not reoccur. Toyota, the car manufacturer, take this principle into their meetings and have a *hansei-kai* (reflection meeting) to review what went wrong.

They do this even if a project is executed well. If someone claims that there were not any problems with the project, they are told that 'no problem is a problem' because it means they have not critically evaluated the project to find opportunities for improvement.

In Summer 2019, my wife and I went to a car dealership to buy a second hand car. It had been advertised on the internet and we had reserved it and travelled two hours to test drive it and purchase it. There was much that was positive about the experience.

- The sales person had phoned back when he said he would prior to us going.
- Sales people were friendly and helpful.
- We were offered a tea and coffee whilst waiting.
- The car was as described.
- The salesperson ensured that it was parked in an easy place ready to test drive.

However, I wonder if they ever really ask their customers for open and honest, critical consideration feedback. If they did they would know that:

- The customer car park was full up with dealer cars and so nowhere to park. Important at all times for a customer, but especially when you need to use the toilet after a 2-hour car journey!

- The appearance of a '£99 admin fee' on the bill, when there was no mention of this on their website, was very frustrating as it was an additional cost.

- The long list of upselling of warranty, alloy wheel, puncture and paint cover is frustrating, and should start with a question like, "Would you be interested in items that might save you money and protect elements of your car purchase?" to save the customer feeling like a cash cow. (To be fair to the sales person, he was not pushy and was a good advert to the company.)

Unless they get that honest feedback, they can miss crucial improvements needed and it could impact on the next customer attending (because they can't park) or pull out of the deal (because they are annoyed with the surprise admin fee). If they were to look strategically at how to improve they may focus on the wrong improvements because they don't have all the information. I always recommend that, wherever possible, leaders involve their stakeholders in this review. Customer surveys and feedback scores give you an indication as to how your business is coming across.

Proposal

"I have a dream that my four little children will one day live in a nation where they will not be judged by the colour of their skin, but by the content of their character. I have a dream today!"

These are the infamous words of Martin Luther King, part of his speech on 23rd August 1963 from the steps of the Lincoln Memorial in Washington, D.C. Even this one sentence makes clear his dream for equality in American society. When you read or listen to the whole speech, you are left with no doubt what destination he hoped for. And that is what a good leader does with their dream, vision, hope and destination. They paint a clear picture of what they want to get to. Seth Godin, in his book Tribes, says, "The secret of leadership is simple: Do what you believe in. Paint a picture of the future. Go there. People will follow."

But how do you give a clear picture? Does it need to be in a speech on steps like Martin Luther King? I think you need 4 key aspects:

- Simple
- Real
- Marker points
- Live it

Simple

"It'll look something like that," said my friend Julian, as he handed me the envelope where he had drawn out his initial plan for his house. Julian had built three houses for his family now. He was very good at it. He had an immense talent at building and carpentry, and built to a very high standard. He was able to envision what the crumbled shell or building plot could look like, but it all started with a simple drawing.

When crafting our vision, our message needs to be simple. If you can't say it in a sentence then it's not simple and people won't remember it. In December 2018 I was working with a school that was struggling. The headteacher knew that it needed to improve, but in talking to him and the senior team, he was not clear about what they actually wanted. So I asked them two questions: "What's your purpose? If it was all working well what would it look like?" They talked about what they passionately wanted for vulnerable children and the sort of things that they would do to help them. And then I summarised what they had said. We chatted and refined that summary until we came up with Know, Show, Grow.

- Get to know the children, their needs and their starting points.
- Show them learning behaviours.
- Grow them through experiences designed for them.

Real

Avoid fluff and fudging the issue. Bring clarity and precision. Politics and social media can have a lot of spin doctoring, fake news and over-dramatisation. People want a picture of a future that is better than the present but they also want the journey based on a realistic starting point. If there is an issue, be clear and specific on it but don't over-inflate it.

For example, “We have a downward trend of 15% over the last 3 years and we need to look at XXX” is clear about the problem. “We need to improve to be in the top 25% in 3 years” is clear about the journey. No fluff or fudge, just clarity of where you are now and where you want to be.

Marker points

Julian’s back of an envelope plan now has a full A1 size detailed drawing. But this end goal diagram will never come to fruition without his Gantt chart. This is a type of timeline grid that illustrates a project schedule with tasks to be performed and time intervals when they are happening. Everyone is clear when reading this as to what needs to be done by key dates.

For really big issues, you may need to give the end vision but outline key marker points of stepping-stones that you want to achieve. What does this look like in the next week, month, year, 5 years? Paint the pictures of each stage.

Live it

Martin Luther King may have stood on those steps and told about his dream, but each day he lived it. Living your dream means you model it in the way you speak and act. You talk about it at every opportunity. When you see it in your building you ‘Spot, Speak and Synergise’ it. You spot the practice, speak to them about it and synergise it with what you are always talking about. Remember the difference between filling the bath with a torrent from the tap or filling it by a dripping tap. In truth you need both – the big speak events and the constant drip, drip, drip of what you are looking for.

Priority

So you've done the review. You know what is working and what isn't. You've done the visioning and you know what it looks like when you get there. And there is a gap. In fact there are several gaps. In fact quite a few areas that need improving. And so you list them all and you get the team to frantically work on them all. And then, pretty quickly either burnout or frustration come because you have too many things to work on. The key at this point is 'priority'. Which one or two things are you going to prioritise? Any more than that and you reduce the impact or dilute the vision.

Partners

Julian's third house (and final one if you speak to him and his wife Tracy now) was nearing completion. They were sort of moved in, with snagging and finishing items needed, and a lot of landscaping. So, he had lots to do that morning as he rushed around the back garden. It was not in his plan for him to fall and severely cut his leg open. It was not in his plan to spend hours in surgery and days in hospital. It was not in his plan to lose the full function of his leg. And so now his plan needed partners to help him complete his house and garden. Whilst he sat with his leg elevated, out of action, out came the back of the envelope again, only this time it was to make a list. A list of people he knew and those he needed to get the job complete.

The same applies to us when aiming for our goal. We are very unlikely to be able to achieve the goal all by ourselves. The trick is to get the right people focussing on the right things for you. You need IN, OUT and OVER people to help you get to your destination.

- IN – Who have you got on the team that is right to lead and shape these areas?
- OUT – Who do you know that you need to bring on board to help develop this area?
- OUT – Who do you need to get to know to help develop things? What skills are you looking for?
- OVER – Who will oversee this? Who will be your governance to oversee, challenge and support?

Plan

Next comes the real planning. Plan some simple, clear steps that will get you there. Plot who does each step and when it needs to be done by. What are the costs that are involved in terms of money, time involvement? What will each step look like when it is successful?

If you're looking to employ a new member of staff, the passage you would take can be as simple as:

- Review the staff structure to see what is needed
- Draw up a job description and person specification
- Examine advertising options
- Advertise the post
- Allocate people to show prospective candidates around
- Prepare interview task and questions
- Invite panel for interview
- Allocate rooms for interviews and tasks

Next to each of these you would place any costs, dates and who is responsible.

Keep it alive

But of course all of this planning can lead to nothing, unless you keep it alive and have fanatical follow through. Plan regular times of review where you give each other permission to hold each other to account for reaching the steps in the plan. When a goal is not met, then ask each other the question, "What can I do to help you achieve that action?" There then comes the fine balance in your review that there may need to be some flexibility. Sometimes, you head off in a direction, only to discover that there is a change in circumstance or situation. Plans, therefore, should be 'written in soft clay' not etched in hard stone, to allow you to adapt or tweak direction when circumstances change.

But, through it all, whatever stage you are at, it is crucial that you and key leaders live out the vision and destination every day.

Have a Strategic Perspective
1
Purpose
VISION
2
Starting point
Hansei Kai
"ALL THE RIGHT PIECES FOR SUCCESS"
ROAD CLOSED
3
DREAM VISION
HOPE
Destination
a) Simple
b) Real
c) Marker points
d) Live it
CLARITY
FUTURE
4
Focus
DON'T DILUTE THE VISION
ONE OR TWO THINGS
5
Partners
IN. OUT. OVER
6
Key steps
REVIEW
©Everyday People/©Jane Ryder

Personal Reflection – Strategic Perspective

Strategic thinking		
Consider what you are working on at the moment. Complete the strategic journey plan.		
Area	**Key Question**	**Thoughts**
Purpose	***What is your vision? What are the 3 core values?***	
Starting point	***Where am I now? What is working? What is not working?***	
Destination	***What do I want it to look like?***	
Focus	***What 1 or 2 things do I need to focus on?***	
Partners	***Who can help me to get there? What skills do I need?***	
Key steps	***What do I need to do?***	

Personal Reflection – Strategic Perspective

Destination		
How clear are you on your destination?		
Area	Key Question	Thoughts
Simple	*What is it in a sentence?*	
Real	*What is it in 3 words?*	
Marker Points	*What are my key markers of success?*	
Live it	*When have I used 'Spot, Speak and Synergise'?*	

Keep it alive
Plans should be flexible, to allow you to adapt or tweak direction when circumstances change. What do you need to be willing to adjust?

Chapter 9: Problem Solve

Norman

"When we face a problem, we tend to jump into identifying the immediate solution for it. Do this and you can sometimes miss the root of the problem and end up potentially just papering over cracks."

No ordinary man

Nothing I write in this book will do justice to Norman Savory. Now, you may not have heard of Norman, but he was an amazing man. He served in the medical section of the RAF in the second world war and on his return from the war he worked as an engineer for Firestones, a tyre manufacturer, to keep the manufacturing machines operating. Redundancy in the 1970s led him to work for Trico, a plastics company, doing a similar job until his retirement in the mid-1980s. Throughout all of this he was a founding member of a small congregational church in Stanwell, near Heathrow Airport. As a volunteer, he helped the church start from a small group meeting in a tin shack to a large congregation meeting in a purpose-built church building.

Maybe this all sounds quite ordinary, and to many maybe Norman was an ordinary, decent man. But to me, he was an absolute hero. You see, Norman was my grandad. As a child, his sandcastle and sand-boat building was the highlight of every summer holiday. But as I grew older, and spent time watching his ability to rewire a house and fix anything we broke as children, I became acutely aware of his immense ability to problem solve. If something broke, he was able to examine the damage, evaluate different ways to solve the problem and choose the most efficient way of doing it. Almost always, it involved using the immense array of pots and tins that held every conceivable bolt, screw and 'that will come in handy later' item.

Now, of course I am biased about my grandad. He is, after all, my grandad. But I also could see an immense problem-solving brain. He taught me the power of washing-up liquid as a lubricant for squeaky door hinges.

He taught me how to solder and he taught me how to use a tap and die to create new screw threads on things. There was literally nothing he could not fix, including a Chrysler Avenger engine that I inadvertently managed to blow up on the M25 in 1987! But the most important thing he taught me was to slow down, not rush, weigh up the options and then choose the best approach. He taught me that problem solving comes in 6 key questions:

- What is working?
- What is not working?
- What is causing the problem?
- What are the different ways of solving the problem?
- Which out of these ideas is the most efficient way of solving it?
- Which way is cost-efficient too?

When we face a problem, we tend to jump into identifying the immediate solution for it. Do this and you can sometimes miss the root of the problem and end up potentially just papering over cracks.

When Norman Savory worked on the 1972 Chrysler Avenger, he knew it was smoking, he knew the engine was misfiring. He could see that there was water and oil mixing. The obvious answer was the head gasket. But Norman had learnt never to jump to the immediately obvious cause. What if he fixed that and put the engine back together and there was still a problem? He knew all possible problems had to be investigated before deciding what action to take. As it turned out, the piston rings, big end shells and the head gasket all needed fixing or replacing. I had blown the engine on it good and proper. For many, the car would have just been scrapped, but remember this was Norman Savory, problem solver and machinist!

Now, you may be thinking that you didn't want to read a Haynes manual on how to fix a Chrysler Avenger. And this is not the purpose here, to explain car mechanics. The purpose is to help us develop how we problem solve.

- Establish our current position & what might be causing any problems.
- Fully evaluate ways forward.
- Plan carefully to implement.
- Review how it has worked and plan next steps.

So let's look in more detail as to how you can evaluate the current position. I have a model that I use that I call Skate, Flow, Dig.

Skate

Firstly, skate over your organisation or situation. This is about a quick glance of the data that you hold, people that can give you feedback (customers, staff, external stakeholders - both informal chats and formal surveys), what you see in your venue (environment condition, signage, display) and any paperwork (*eg*, timetables, handouts). After this, consider what story it is telling you. What is your hypothesis at this point?

Flow

The flow line is examining an issue across the organisation. From your skate over the organisation, there will be an area of concern that you want to check. For example, if you felt decoration was poor, then look at the decoration in each room and compare key areas. Was it just the one area or a consistent problem? If you felt it was staff behaviour, then look at the behaviour in each department.

I was working with a school, looking at science. The skate over the school raised an issue around how scientific enquiry and investigation was taught. So we took a flow line and looked at each year group in the school, at books, displays, teacher interview and planning. This enabled us to see if it was across the school or in pockets.

Dig

Having looked at an issue across your organisation, you may have a more refined area of concern. It is now time to dig down deeper and look at the root cause of what might be causing this. So, if your flow line was looking at staff behaviour, then your flow line may have narrowed this down to newly-appointed staff. Now is the time to dig down into this area. Hold some more detailed interviews to discover what the cause is. Is it poor induction on the standards expected? Is it that the standards were not clear at advertising the jobs? Is it that standards are not regularly revisited?

In the school that was looking at science, we identified all but one year group had an issue in the quality of teaching scientific enquiry. Digging down deeper with each teacher identified that teachers were not confident in what needed to be taught. There was not a clear progression document explaining what needed to be taught at each stage. Digging down allowed the leader to see that teacher training and a clear progression document was needed.

Skate asks the question, "What do I see?" Flow asks the question, "Is there a pattern?" Dig asks the question, "What might be causing it?" By following this series of questions, you have a clearer view on what to improve.

Blind men and elephants

There is an ancient religious story of blind men and an elephant. A group of blind men have never encountered an elephant before and so they sit at different parts of the elephant and touch it and try to describe to each other what an elephant is from their limited experience. Of course, for each one it is a different experience. The moral of the story is that humans have a tendency to claim absolute truth based on their limited, subjective experience, ignoring or refuting other equally limited but maybe helpful perspectives. It is only when all of the perspectives are put together that you can maybe get the full picture. Social media is awash with this limited view and the echo chambers that then ensue as we seek people who 'look at the elephant the same way that we do'. If we approach problem-solving from just one perspective, our limited view can be our downfall. We need to look for a 360-degree, 'full body scan' of the problem.

Meta Mirror

As a coach, one of the techniques I use with clients is the 'Meta Mirror'. This is trying to look at the problem from another person's point of view. Sometimes this entails actually moving seats and sitting in their seat and looking at the problem from their angle. We need to employ the meta mirror on our problem. So, if we are looking at staff behaviour, sit in the chair of a newly employed person. What was it like looking at the advert? What was their induction like? What are meetings like for them? Is the right media being used to communicate with them? Of course, the best way is to actually ask them in an open and honest forum.

When applying this principle, consider each person involved. What perspective do they have on the problem? How important would they score it out of 10?

Let's take an issue of 'the main office is cold'.

You, the boss: You pop in occasionally. You don't feel the cold. It feels a little chilly. You think it is a 3/10 problem.

Muriel, the secretary: She is in there 8 hours a day. She feels the cold. She had caught several colds and has been off sick for 20 days this year. She has resorted to thick socks and thermals. She sees it as a 10/10 problem.

Fred, the finance lead: He doesn't feel the cold but he is fed up with Muriel off sick with colds. He is fed up with her moaning about the cold. Some staff try to sneak in heaters from home and this has increased the electric bill. He is concerned about the cost of this. He sees it as an 8/10 problem.

Jane, the rep: She is only in for 3 mornings as she is often out on the road. When she is in it's a bit chilly and she is concerned for Muriel sitting in it all the time. She sees it as a 7/10 problem.

You see it as a 3 out of 10 problem. But take Muriel, Fred and Jane's scores of 10, 8 and 7 and the average of that is 7 out of 10. Your staff have it as a problem of concern much higher than you. Now you take their ideas into account as to what is causing it and what ideas they have for helping solve it. Involving them helps you understand the situation better and helps them take ownership of the solution. Seeing it from their perspective helps you gain that 360-degree scan of the issues and know what the problems actually are. *Eg*, drafty windows and doors, rather than paying for a new boiler and radiators and still not solving the problem.

Coaching you to growth

Norman Savory's 6 key questions are leadership gems. They are about taking time to process, examine the real root cause and then plan possible solutions, refining them to find the ultimate solution. This same approach can be found in the basic GROW coaching method used to help people find solutions to their problems. This approach, first documented by John Whitmore in Coaching for Performance, outline 4 key stages:

G – What is your **goal?**
R – What is the **reality?** Good and bad.
O – What are your **options?**
W – Which of these options is the best one to solve the problem?

Compare the two approaches and see the synergy.

Norman's questions	Coaching
	G – What is your goal?
What is working?	R – What is the reality? Good and bad.
What is not working?	
What is causing the problem? (Examine all possibilities)	
What are the different ways of solving the problem?	O – What are your options?
Which out of these ideas is the most efficient way of solving it?	W – Which of these options is the best one to solve the problem?
Which way is cost-efficient too?	

Problem solving is essentially about coaching yourself through the situation. The more you practise this approach, the more it becomes second nature. You can even use it when there is seemingly no time and a decision is needed instantly.

Stress & problem solving

When we are faced with a problem, it causes stress. Stress releases a chemical hormone called cortisol. Cortisol affects the hippocampus, the area of the brain involved with memory, learning, and emotional regulation. Therefore, the ability to solve a problem and think creatively is diminished. When trying to solve a problem, you need to reduce cortisol. Three things that can help reduce cortisol are:

- Exercise
- Quiet
- Thankfulness

Therefore, it is crucial when trying to solve a problem to give yourself some time. Don't rush in; there is a high chance with a big stressful problem that your cognitive problem solving is inhibited. So when you find yourself getting stuck and frustrated, stop. Go for a walk, have a moment alone in quiet. You will notice as well that Norman's first question is not 'What is not working?' but 'What is working?' This position of thankfulness gives a positive, cortisol-reducing base to start from. It also allows you to narrow down the problem.

Approaches to problem solving

Many people rush straight into an off-the-shelf solution. "What has someone else done? I will use that." That is one approach but always taking that means that we can miss something even better or something that could cause a problem in our context. There are 6 basic approaches to problem solving:

Analytical	Evaluates detail and what is missing.
Logical	Evaluates where the problem is. Uses historical or similar solutions.
Creative	Envisions several outcomes. Creates unique pathways.
Positive	Open minded & collaborative. Not restricted by past results.
Absolute	Sees the black & white of a problem. Looks for an authoritative source for an answer.
Rational	Deduces an optimal solution from the thinker's perspective.

Each one has its strengths and weaknesses but used in combination they can be incredibly powerful. If we were to approach a problem by asking key questions in each problem-solving field, it should allow us to gain a much clearer picture of a) the situation, b) options, c) strengths and weaknesses of an option and d) which way is best to go forward.

Analytical	What do I have? What is missing?
Logical	What am I trying to achieve? (Big picture) What has been used before that might help?
Creative	What are the different options? (Multi-solution approach below.)
Positive	What other things can I consider? Who can I collaborate with?
Absolute	What are the pros and cons of each situation? What does the authoritative source in this area have to say on it?
Rational	What is the optimal solution from my perspective?

I have a proforma that I use and ask these questions when tackling a problem. Just 1 minute spent on each one can open up new ways of thinking about solutions. You can find this on the Everyday Leader website in the book resources section.

Multi-solution approach

Mr Price was my Design Technology teacher at secondary school. He drove a Lotus Europa sports car, wore the archetypal white Design Technology lab coat and was scary. He loved designing and making, but you daren't put a foot wrong in his class or he would get cross with you. Despite that, I could see that there was something to learn from him about designing and making. So, I kept my head down and was able to learn an approach that not only helped me with DT but is part of the key problem-solving approach for situations I faced as a leader.

It works like this. When we have a problem, the tendency is to stick to the norm to solve it. Often, the same solution can cause the same problems. By thinking wider, we open up to a solution that may avoid the usual problems.

The creative solution approach is set out below.

Establish the problem	Possible solutions	Analyse solutions	Decide on the solution
What problem needs to be solved?	What are all the possible ways of solving it? However unlikely the ideas may seem, write them down.	Which of these could work?	Which are the most cost-effective?
		Which of these are viable or feasible?	Which have the greatest impact?
		Can any hybrid idea be formed from the aspects that could work?	Which of these offer the best solution?

So, I used that in my 1985 Design Technology lessons to make a new type of slide projector for my O level project. Now I may have just lost a large number of readers who are now asking, "What is a slide projector?" Try Googling it; it's what we used before laptops and video projectors. But this problem-solving process is not to be just discarded in 1980s history and placed in the loft where my slide projector still sits. I use that same process to solve problems that I face as a leader.

Whilst a headteacher, one of the biggest headaches was covering a teacher when they would be absent for a few weeks or more. Covering any member of staff can be difficult, but a teacher had 30 children who would still turn up tomorrow and need teaching. The automatic answer was 'get a cover teacher in'. Good supply teachers are super members of the team. However, some struggled to manage some of the children in my school and sometimes created more problems than they solved and parental complaints then followed.

So, whenever someone needed covering, we would bring out this multi-solution process. We would look at pros and cons of each decision and then look at what was the best solution in this circumstance. Sometimes an initial idea could be used in full and sometimes it could be mixed with another idea to make a hybrid idea. You can do it on a piece of scrap paper or create a grid as below:

Option	**Cover teacher**	**Use school Part-time teacher**	**Use a Higher Level Teaching Assistant**		**Head/deputy covers**
Positive	Trained teacher.	Know the children. Good quality. Good if both part-time teachers can help creating one whole person.	Know the children. Good quality.		Know the children. Good quality.
Negative	Don't know the children. Quality recently has been lower.	Can they cover long term? Impact on other class.	Qualified	Unqualified	Impact on leadership & school
Names		Betty	Wilma	Barnie	
Possibility	Medium	Strong	Strong	Medium	No – too much negative impact on school development.
Full/ hybrid	Full or Hybrid	Full	Full	Hybrid	
Preference	3	1	2		No
Next step	Investigate availability & quality available	Investigate availability	Investigate availability		

Now there are more possibilities you could list above, but it gives you the basic idea of the process. If you can, sitting down with a couple of people to come up with the ideas often helps you widen the ideas.

You can apply this approach to most decisions. Should I employ another staff member? Should I get a loan to expand the business? What should I do about this struggling staff member? What should I do about staff development in my company?

So let's take one of them: 'What shall I do about this struggling staff member?' There are perhaps two immediate, 'normal' ways of approaching this. 1) Put them through professional development that will support them to improve. 2) Review their performance and if they are not up to the standard required of the job, take them through capability procedures. This can lead to them being dismissed from their post if they don't improve to the required standard. These are both options. But are there others?

Let me take you through the process.

Options

Firstly, list as many options as possible, even if you think they are a bit unlikely. If you can do this with another person it can spark creativity, bring a different perspective, and may help reduce any bias that you might have. Here are some examples below. You may think of more. If you do, then just get another bit of paper!

Option	Positive	Negative	Names	Possibility	Full/ Hybrid	Preference
CPD training						
Capability & dismiss them if don't improve						
Provide a mentor						
Move to a different role						
Set clear targets & review						
Be tough on them and hope they leave						
Make their role redundant						
Ask them what the issue is and what could help to resolve it						

You will notice that in our initial options, there are some that I would certainly not promote at all. 'Be tough on someone and hope they leave' and 'Make their role redundant' are weak responses that indicate poor HR and leadership character. They are both fudging the issue and in the case of 'Make their role redundant' can create further operational problems. Formally dismissing someone should not be taken lightly; we are dealing with human beings and any dismissal should be after due process, offering support and trying to develop the person.

As a leader we have a moral responsibility to follow HR employee processes, ensuring their human rights are honoured. When it comes to this initial stage of idea creation, you can consider ideas, but in your 'negative review' and 'possibility' you should reflect on the morality and ethics of any decision. Your moral character as a leader should be a key driver in decision making. Your character is who walks through the door when no-one is looking. Doing the right thing, even if no-one is around to scrutinise. On issues like staff competency, your HR department should always be consulted and listened to.

Review – Positive & Negative

The next stage is the hardest part; looking at the positives and negatives of each idea. You will have natural 'confirmation bias' where you will want to err towards a solution. For example, you might want to dismiss them because you think they are a bit lazy, or you may want to move them to a different role because it might solve some tension in that team. The important thing here is to try to remain objective. Try to think of the person as nameless so that personal feelings do not come into it. Try to work with someone that you know will challenge your bias and look at things from a different perspective. Try not to dismiss any ideas or discuss them at this point. Just put down the review points. A key aspect of this review will be considering whether the action supports the core purpose of the organisation. For example, in a school, does it support the development of the children? For any organisation, is it in line with your core values?

So, let's take 'dismiss them' as an example.
Positives could be:

- It removes the weakness.
- Sends a strong signal out on what is expected.

Negatives could be

- It is damaging to the person who is dismissed, especially if due process and support has not been given.

- It creates an immediate gap on the team that might take a while to fill.
- Any area where due process has not been followed could be liable for an unfair dismissal claim.
- Dismissal is unsettling for others. It can create a 'high threat' culture.

There will be many other points, I am sure, but this should give you the idea.

Names

This is for who might be involved in this. This is helpful for reviewing the possibility of your proposed solution. If the people you have allocated to assist are already snowed under, it then forms part of your decision-making process. It doesn't stop you taking it, but helps you determine the implications of any potential decisions and consider how you reduce any negative impact. In the example above of the struggling member of staff, if you have someone down to be a mentor, but they are already snowed under with work, then you either pick a different mentor or adjust some of the mentor's workload.

Possibility

This is where you decide how possible it is. Is it a 'strong', 'medium', 'low' or 'no'?

Factors that help decide if it is a 'no' include:

- It is not moral or ethical.
- The benefits are completely outweighed by the negatives.
- It will cause more damage in other areas than the benefits gained in the area you are working on.

Low options will mean:

- The positive outweighs the negative but only just.
- It has hardly any impact on the situation. At best, it is just a holding solution.

Medium options will mean:

- There are some negatives, but any negative impact on other areas of the organisation is relatively small.
- There will be positive impact on the situation although it does not solve every area.

Strong options will mean:

- There are no negatives or virtually none.
- You can see it will have a significantly positive impact on the situation.

Once you have weighed up each option, you look first to find strong options. If you are lucky to have more than one, then you look for the one that a) has least impact on other areas and b) that gains best consensus from your senior team. If you have no strong options, then a medium can be considered. These are likely to be short-term solutions as there is negative impact on other areas. Low options are unlikely to be used unless your back is against the wall. If you're facing using a 'low option', my recommendation is to get out another piece of paper and think again, or seek outside consultation on your options; to think wider.

Full/hybrid

This allows you to consider whether there are any aspects of a weaker idea that could be combined with other ideas to create a hybrid solution. In the example of the weaker member of staff, it could be that taking a bit of the 'send on a course or other CPD', 'set targets' and 'mentor' could create a stronger hybrid solution.

Bias & team

Problem solving is not easy; the clue is in the title. We may not have encountered this problem before and, even if we have, it doesn't mean the same solution will work this time as there are often people and situation factors that affect the issue. Problem solving requires a blend of creative and logical thinking. However, one of the biggest problems that affects our ability to think creatively is our human brain and the way that it can be impeded by our emotions. We have a logical thinking part of the brain, the frontal cortex, but we also have the amygdala – the emotional centre of the limbic system. Our emotional part can stimulate bias – a tendency to want to prove ourselves right with a solution we already lean towards (confirmation bias). If our problem involves people, there will be a bias towards those whom we have better relationship with.

So when you are facing an important problem to solve, I recommend two steps.

Firstly, if you can, involve other senior team members in your thinking through of the problem using the grid structure above. Each team member will have a bias, but between you all you will spot and highlight or question each other's bias more easily than spotting and challenging your own. Also, as a collective, you will bring more ideas to the table. If you really want to come up with clarity, consider asking a trusted member of the team who has first-hand experience on the shop floor.

Secondly, if you recognise too much bias, even as a team, or if the problem is really complex, involve either a coach or a consultant to help bring objectivity to the issue. Just as my grandad taught me that washing up liquid helps free up squeaky door hinges, an objective, external view can free up the resistance caused by bias.

Review & repeat

Problem solving is not like the movies. In the movie the solution works and the hero rides off into the sunset. In reality, a good problem solver reviews how the solution to the problem is going. Is it working? You review it using a series of questions:

- What is working well?
- What is not working quite so well?
- Do any adjustments need to be made?
- Is it working so poorly that a complete solution needs to be found?

You then go through the process again of problem solving. If only a small part is not working, then you focus on the small part to find a solution. If there are multiple factors, then it could be that the right solution on paper has not come to fruition in reality. And so the process begins again. As a leader, this can be frustrating, but that is where perseverance and tenacity come in.

Problem Solve
No ordinary man
1
Establish current position and what might be causing any problems
negative
positive
thankfulness
analytical
logical
creative
positive
absolute
rational
What's missing?
Look at the big picture
Multi, solution approach
Other things to consider
collaborate?
Pros / Cons
Optimal solution
What is working?
2
Fully evaluate ways forward
G goal
R REALITY
O options
W? Which one
MORAL CHARACTER
3
Plan carefully to implement
CALENDAR
4
Review how it worked and plan next steps
©Everyday People / ©Jane Ryder

Personal Reflection – Problem Solve

Your approach
How do you find solving problems? What do you find difficult about solving a problem?
What bias do you recognise has entered your thinking recently?

Problem solving resources & planning sheets can be found **on** www.everydayleader.co.uk/everydaybookresources **.**

Personal Reflection – Problem Solve

GROW approach
Think about a problem that you faced recently. Think about it using the GROW approach.
G – What is your goal?
R – What is the reality?
Working
Not working
Causing problems
O – What are your options?
W – Which of these options is the best one to solve the problem?

Chapter 10: Drive for results

Susan and Anna

"A great leader has vision. They know clearly what they want the end result to look like. They can see it in their mind's eye, they can smell it, taste it. They have a metaphorical fridge with a picture on it. They have a dream, like Martin Luther King, that is etched in glorious technicolour on their very soul. If you want to get others on board to get the result, it is a picture that you will take out daily and share with those around you, so that they too can envisage the goal. The hardest step, is then to have the courage to take the journey. Courage needs to be continuous."

No ordinary woman

One of the greatest privileges that I have had was my trip to Kenya in 2015 to see the work of Emerging Leaders' Leadership for Life programme. Emerging Leaders recognise that in the poorest communities of the world, people need more than being given grain. People need more than being taught how to farm. People need to be taught how to lead themselves with the challenges that they face. Leadership for Life teaches people how to recognise poverty thinking and replace it with leadership mindsets. Underpinning all of this is the importance of leading not for yourself but for others.

As we drove to the spot outside of Navaisha in Kenya, the views from the roadside slowly rolled by. Streetside sellers, dusty tracks, makeshift roadside sales points, gradually easing to Kenyan countryside. The car slowed, and turned off onto what was dried mud and builders' rubble, and we climbed a small hill into a field. John and Anna, our Kenyan guides, who had now become good friends, pointed ahead to the concrete-block building, clearly unfinished. To the naked eye, it was just a half-finished building site. But to me, it was a miracle. It was testimony to one very hard-working woman, Susan Wasike.

Susan, one year earlier, had completed the Leadership for Life programme. One leadership mindset was key for Susan; the mindset of 'see and take responsibility'. This mindset is learning to see things that are not ok and take responsibility for them. On completing the Leadership for Life course with Emerging Leaders, Susan, an administrator in a flower and veg growing company, saw things with new eyes. One thing that really resonated with Susan is that she saw young girls having to walk for miles to attend senior school.

She felt that this was unacceptable because of their safety and it restricted access for some girls to attend school. She had no money, no resources, no experience of building or running a school. But she knew that she had to take responsibility for it. She discovered, through her local church, that there was some land donated to the church for a girls' school. But there was no money to build it. So she set about enlisting the help of other church members to raise money, source materials and hassle builders to build it. So, as I looked at this school building, it was testament to a woman driven by results.

We entered the building, and as a UK headteacher visiting their school, I was treated as royalty. But it was not me who was royalty. . . I was about to meet real royalty. I met the girls, I met the headteacher and I also had the privilege of meeting Susan. It is Susan that is educational royalty. She was an everyday Kenyan lady, but she had a vision and a passion for building the legacy of a local senior school for girls. She is known by some as 'The Lioness'. She is truly an everyday leader.

Anna

"Sorry I'm late," said Anna as she plonked down her large handbag on the chair next to me. Anna turned to the waitress and ordered her usual 'Lady Grey' tea. Anna was always busy, but Anna is not a high-powered posh executive. Anna is a driven headteacher, who has worked with schools in challenging circumstances.

To us, the triad of headteachers that worked closely together, she was known affectionately as 'Lady Anna of Halifax'. Her penchant for Lady Grey tea gave her the title and 'Halifax' as she was the headteacher of a primary school of the same name. Anna was our friend and colleague and together we shaped each other's thinking on education.

Anna had a good heart but was also driven. She knew what she wanted for her children and had high expectations for her staff. I'm sure, at times, working for her was scary as her expectations were so high. I secretly think sometimes she even scared herself with her drive. All of our schools had their challenges, due to the catchments of pupils that they served, but it was Anna who drove standards faster. She knew what she wanted the education to look like and passionately encouraged her team to achieve that. She is now no longer a headteacher but has taken on the CEO role creating a multi-academy trust of six schools, including her former school, Halifax. Her journey continues with the schools in the Trust and with those she collaborates with more widely.

Key Components

So what helps you strive for results, whether it is building a school, increasing profit or raising standards? Let me introduce you to the 5 Ds a leader needs to drive for results well whilst caring for and developing your staff in the process.

- Determination
- Direction
- Drive
- Delivery
- Development

Determination

Meet anyone who achieves great things and it is their dogged determination that is evident. Whether Susan with a school from scratch, Anna getting school results or Nelson Mandela changing thinking in a nation, all of them are determined. The determination starts from the root of the cause.

Clear purpose that resonates

There has to be a clear purpose, one that resonates with you. For Susan it was the inequality for girls' education in Navaisha in Kenya. For Anna it was wanting the best education to create life opportunities for all children in her schools. When challenges come, when results don't meet expectation, when the project hits a snag, it is the resonating purpose that gives determination. But that purpose alone does not prescribe the journey.

Vision

A great leader knows clearly what they want the end result to look like. They can see it in their mind's eye, they can smell it, taste it. They have a metaphorical fridge with a picture on it. They have a dream, like Martin Luther King, that etched is in glorious technicolour on their very soul. If you want to get others on board to get the result, it is a picture that you will take out daily and share with those around you, so that they too can envisage the goal.

Courage

The hardest step is then to have the courage to take the journey. Courage needs to be continuous. The day you take the first step and tell your first person your dream takes courage to risk sharing the dream and risk derision. It takes courage to meet head on the challenges that threaten to derail it. It takes courage to keep going when tired and exhausted. It takes courage to take the decision to hand part of it or all of it on to someone else because it needs some new thinking or energy. Taking the step is difficult; you feel the fear and the 'what ifs'. Courage is feeling the fear and doing it anyway.

Direction

Strategy

One of the things that drives people mad when working for someone is when ideas come fast and furious but there is no clear strategy. For results to be achieved and for people to join with you, you need to have a clear strategic overview:

- What is our current position?
- What is our end goal?
- What is the gap?
- What is the one thing we are working on to get us closer to where we want to be?

Clear and focused goals

You need goals in order to know if you have been successful in achieving your results. Chris McChesny, in his book 4 Disciplines of Execution[xxi], stresses the importance of not having too many, though. He suggests having just two or three – what he calls Wildly Important Goals (WIG) – and that any more than this means that you don't achieve them all well. People struggle to hold more than three things in their head, so to work on more than three goals means they will struggle to remember them, let alone keep the energy focus.

Many of you will know that any goal or target needs to be SMART:

Specific	(simple, sensible, significant)
Measurable	(meaningful, motivating)
Achievable	(agreed, attainable)

Relevant (reasonable, realistic and resourced, results-based)

Time-bound (time-based, time limited, time/cost limited, timely, time-sensitive)

Chris McChesny helpfully explains that a goal needs to be a) focused on lead (or input) measures and b) focused on getting from X to Y by Z.

Lead measures are the things that you actually do that can be measured. So, if you are a teacher and you want to raise boys' reading standards, your focus needs to be on what you can influence, *eg*, how often they read and what they read. Here is what that might look like:

We will increase the number of 10-minute boy-friendly texts they read each week from 1 to 5 by 1st January.

You then focus your energy and recording achievement into this area of input. Schools and businesses are often judged on the output. For example, in schools the percentage at national average; in business the percentage of market share or profit. It is valid to look at these, but the focus of energy needs to be on measuring how you are doing in the area that will improvethem. There is the phrase, 'weighing the pig doesn't make it fatter'. What will make the pig fatter is the quality of its food and environment. When the farmer focuses on that, the pig gets fat. It is the same for us when we have a goal - focus your review on the thing you have control over and it will help you reach your goal.

If you are a business, you may want to raise the number of bookings you get for your service. The way this will happen is through conversations with business owners/people who make the bookings. So, your focus could be:

We will increase the number of conversations with companies/bookers each week from 1 to 10 by 1st January.

You then focus your energy and recording achievement in this area of input. Don't just record how many bookings you are getting. Focus your measurement on what you do - the thing you have control over.

Planning

Now you know what you are focused on, you then plan for it. There are all sorts of planning grids out there. The basic principle is:

Focus	Actions	Who	When by	Cost	Success
The key goal that you are focused on. Ideally no more than 2	What you will actually do.	Who is responsible for it.	When it needs to be done by. Include review points.	What it will cost. Money and time.	How you will know that it has been successful.

Plans need to be kept simple. I remember the days as a headteacher where we had our 30-page development plans. These are only good for holding the door open or as a wedge for a wobbly table. People cannot hold all of that information. At the end of my time as a headteacher, we got this down to 2 sides of A4. Sure, you may need some pages with some detail, but the headline plan needs to be clear and simple.

Plans are only good as how often they are reviewed. The core focus of these reviews should not be, "Who has not met their target?"

It should be about reviewing what progress is being made and "What is the best way that we can help you to achieve it?" People need to know that they are held to account, but they also need to know that there is a team of people there to help too.

Drive

Impassion the team

As a leader, we are not only motivating ourselves towards the goal, but a whole team. Therefore, a key component of ensuring there is drive for the project, is to impassion the team. Impassioning is not a one-off event, it is about the daily reminder of the 'why' of what we are doing.

> *"When you know your 'why'. . . your what has more impact, because you are walking in or towards your purpose."* Michael Jr. Comedian

Impassioning is about telling the stories of impact, it's about reminding people about the end goal picture on the metaphorical fridge. Impassioning happens at the photocopier, at the coffee machine, in the elevator as well as in the boardroom.

Regularly endorse high performance

Making people hungry for the project to be successful is key to achieving success. Resonating the goal with their purpose is at the start of this. This is kept alive and a focus by regularly endorsing what high performance and success looks like.
Do this and you will create 'Meerkat Moments'. People, like meerkats, will turn to look at where the noise is and aspire to it.

So, when you give **positive feedback**, where earnt, that will draw attention. Having the **coaching** approach of asking and drawing out 'What is Working Well' (**WWW**) and then considering what could be 'Even Better If' (**EBI**) it was put into action, ensures that people are focused on aiming for the best in every review.

Finally, when you model the high standards of delivery that you expect, it models the expectation that you have. Your delivery to high standards models it to others.

Delivery

Collaboration and delegation

You have the vision etched on your very soul. The danger here is that you then take hold of the brush and paint the picture, when you may need different artists to bring the vision to life. Distributed leadership is so important. Imagine the football team, where the coach tries to play goalie, defender and striker as well as coach the team. . . Madness. Imagine the music conductor, trying to play the flute, cello, drums as well as conduct the orchestra. . . Madness.

If you are going to achieve your vision, you will need others to come with you and help you. You will need to develop a common spirit of collaboration where everyone knows their roles and works for the greater good. You will need to delegate jobs to them and ensure that they carry the authority to get them done. This is done through remembering the following:

Purpose + Alignment = Shift

Alignment

Alignment, and the freedom to delegate better, comes when you:

- Choose those who you know have a heart for what you want to achieve
- Spend time with those you are delegating to, ensuring that they are really clear on the 'why'
- Provide mentors who can help and support
- Give clarity in deadlines with buffer zones, to allow time if there are problems

Development

One of the beautiful things about a great vision or dream is that it not only has the power to affect people positively in its fruition but also in its process. Taking people towards a goal will often mean that there is a lot for people to learn. This gives an amazing opportunity for people to grow as the project evolves. But for this to happen you need to be prepared to equip and develop people. This doesn't happen by accident; it needs a purposeful approach and has three key components:

- Review regularly
- Listen and build trust
- Develop and support others

Share expectation, data updates & analysis regularly

Having worked in education for the last 30 years, I got used to constantly changing goalposts. Just when you thought you were on track, the goalpost changed. Whether it is in education, business or with a charity, your team needs to know where the target is and be reminded of it so it remains the focus of their day-to-day.

As a parent, I remember the car journeys when my children would regularly call out from the back seat, "Are we nearly there yet?" We would then give them a timeframe as to how close we were from our destination. Regular reviews of how we are progressing towards our target is important when working towards a goal.

This review comes in two parts. 1. What does the data tell us? 2. Analyse the data to help understand what next step is needed to reach the goal.

Take the target mentioned earlier for reading improvement in boys:

Increase the number of 10minute boy-friendly texts they read each week from 1 to 5 by 1st January.

Updating staff each week on how many times each child has read on average, allows the team to keep the goal alive, celebrate progress, review what is working and identify what needs to be adapted to increase towards the ultimate goal.

The same applies to the business target example:

Increase the number of conversations with companies/bookers each week from 1 to 10 by 1st January.

Having a chart up to record the conversations and encouraging healthy competition, ensures that the goal remains the focus and progress is celebrated.

It also allows the team to note when someone is struggling with barriers beyond their control or managing their workload, and allows the team to find solutions together. If you leave the review of these factors to the last week, there is little time to respond to the situation, to provide support or make improvements.

I have also learnt the importance of review and celebrating for motivating staff. Working on tricky tasks can feel like gardening and digging manure into a flowerbed. Spend too much time smelling the manure and not taking moments to smell the flowers that have started to grow and you can easily lose motivation. Take time to smell the flowers.

Listen and build trust

Over 30 years of leading in one form or another has drawn me to the same conclusion that my wife had reached within the first year of us being married . . . I don't know it all. She is now doing a jig around the room as she reads this, delighted that her husband of 29 years has finally admitted it. If, as a leader, you fail to realise this, you will do a lot of damage to your project, your team and yourself. As leaders, we know a lot, we have a lot of experience and a lot that helps us with the project at hand. But, if you fail to listen to your team, you will at best miss a helpful improvement or at worst make a fatal error that kills the project. Listening to your team also ensures that they remain involved. When you listen to them, you:

- Hear their experience of the vision
- Hear areas where the project is not working
- Hear gaps in your transferring the passion of the vision

I have a phrase I have used for many years to help my senior leaders understand the value of understanding staff: 'Perception is reality'. Someone's perception may not be 'the reality' but it is 'their reality' and therefore to them, it is the reality. If staff are telling you there are problems, from their perspective, from their reality, then it needs to be weighed up to ensure the project remains on task for everyone.

Listening also has the important benefit of building trust in your team towards you. When they see you listen, weigh up their concerns and feedback your response, it develops trust.

Develop & support others

The bottom line is that there are very few dreams that can be achieved without the help of others. Within an organisation, people make the dream become reality. By having an ethos where you are willing to support them to achieve, you will not only achieve the dream, but you also achieve deep allegiance. Developing others starts from employing people with the core skills needed, assigning them to roles where they work predominantly from their strengths, and then allocating opportunities to them that stretch their experience and comfort zone. Allocating mentors to them, who help them reflect on their experience, allows them to accurately review their performance and target improvement. When you develop people so that they become the best that they can be, in turn, this improves the organisation's performance and standards.

Author's warning

Being driven to your goal is great. However, there is a very dangerous flip side to the coin that you must be aware of and guard yourself against.

Remember that people are people and not resources.

Having vision and having passion is commendable. But, if you are so driven that people become expendable, your leadership has lost its integrity. This comes in many forms, most of which leave nasty stains on people's lives. For example:

- Driving them hard and then disposing of them when they have served their purpose.
- Removing people who seemingly don't seem to align with a new direction of the organisation, without having a discussion with them about the values or skills that they need to develop and giving them time to respond.
- Removing people who ask questions and don't just say yes.
- Manipulating and destroying people to get your own way.

There is a phrase from another context and meaning that could be applied here: "What profits a man if he gains the whole world but loses his soul?" If you achieve your goal but lose the integrity of leadership in the process by losing the value of people, your victory is shallow. Too many lives will have been damaged. The goal is only really achieved if integrity remains intact and people have been taken with you. Like a monarch, you may have the crown and own the land but if the people are no longer with you, what kingdom do you own?

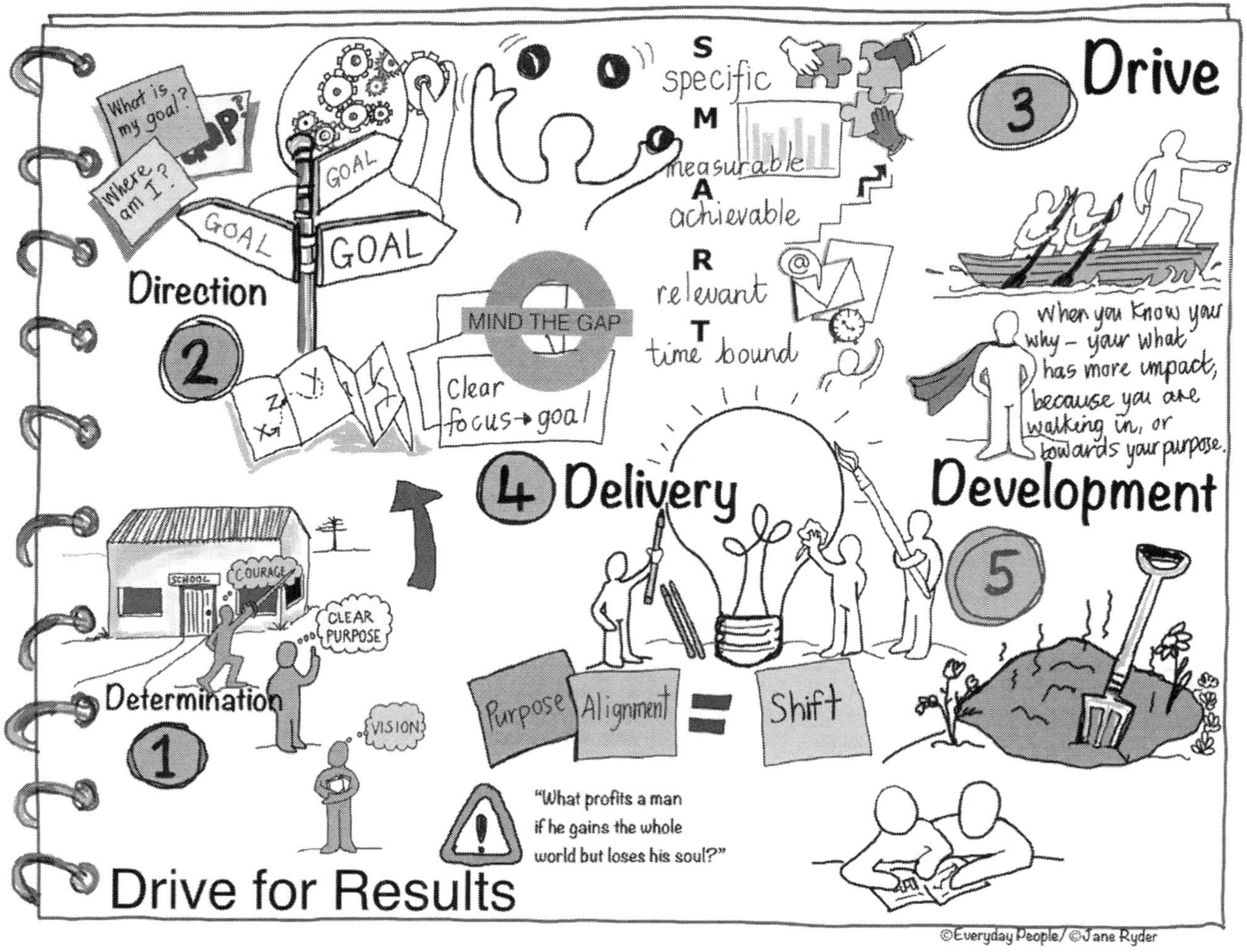
What is my goal?
Where am I?
GOAL
GOAL
GOAL
Direction
2
MIND THE GAP
Clear focus → goal
S
specific
M
measurable
A
achievable
R
relevant
T
time bound
3
Drive
When you know your why – your what has more impact, because you are walking in, or towards your purpose.
4
Delivery
Development
5
SCHOOL
COURAGE
CLEAR PURPOSE
VISION
Determination
1
Purpose
Alignment
=
Shift
"What profits a man if he gains the whole world but loses his soul?"
Drive for Results
©Everyday People/©Jane Ryder

Personal Reflection – Drive for Results

5D Leadership		
Based on what you have read, score yourself out of 10 in each section. Which one thing, from the description in the chapter, do you need to develop to improve it?		
5D Leadership	**Score**	**One thing**
Determination		
Direction		
Drive		
Delivery		
Development		

Personal Reflection – Drive for Results

Direction		
Be focused on getting from X to Y by Z. Take something you are working on at the moment. Can you rephrase it in this way to give you a more specific target?		
From	to	by

Drive	
RAG rate yourself in how you drive improvement	RAG
Share expectation and data regularly	
Listen and build trust	
Develop and support others	
Identify one thing you will do to improve	

Development	
RAG rate yourself in how you drive improvement	RAG
Hear their experience of the vision	
Hear areas where the project is not working	
Hear gaps in your transferring the passion of the vision	
Identify one thing you will do to improve	

Chapter 11: Innovate

David and Simon

"As leaders, we are constantly looking for what is working well and what could be even better, in order to improve our position. The skill of being able to innovate is key to that."

"Welcome to 745. Let me give you all a glass of prosecco. Frankie will take your coat and show you to your table in the Library and Margaret will bring you some canapes."

It could have been a line from any dinner party host or restaurant owner. But these were the instructions from David, a man with an entrepreneurial spirit. On this particular occasion we had managed to secure a table for four at the 745pm restaurant. The principles were simple. You arrived at 7.45pm; you were served a five-course set menu; there was strictly no tipping and you could help yourself to the wine. At the end of the evening David totted up the bottles you had drunk and added the cost, roughly retail, to your bill. In a world full of choice, in a world where restaurants pride themselves in offering a range to their customers, David chose to innovate. He chose to focus on high quality food and create an atmosphere that blended dinner party with restaurant. Friends told him he was mad. "No-one will come out to the countryside." "No-one will come to a restaurant with a set meal. This is not London." The wine importers, when he shared his plan to sell at a little over cost price instead of charging 3 times the cost, also gave him that look of madness. He established his 745 restaurant at Easter 2011; he only opened on Friday and Saturday evening and by Christmas had bookings for 8 weeks ahead.

He closed the restaurant five years later as his 70th birthday approached but still cannot resist opening for an occasional weekend, welcoming back his faithful customers who clamour to get a table. David's innovation in the restaurant business was impressive, but he impresses further when you know his story prior to the 745 restaurant.

David was a chemistry student in the early years of UEA, the East Anglian university whose motto is 'Do Different'. After graduating and training as a hospital administrator he briefly managed High Wycombe District General Hospital and then accepted a post as project manager at one of the London teaching hospitals, looking at new ways to design operating theatres.

In 1975 he left the NHS and started work as a craftsman producing highly original pieces of modern furniture. Having designed a beautiful laminated wooden armchair - Anemone, which was exhibited at the Design Centre in London's Haymarket - he invented a new mechanism for reclining chairs which he incorporated into Anemone to create the Suffolk Recliner, a decidedly different piece of furniture incorporating sailing ropes and bollards. His company went on to make over 5000 of these chairs. It was made under licence in other countries and was voted the iconic piece of British furniture of the 1970s.

A severe recession in 1980 effectively destroyed his business. Out of work, he set about turning himself into a computer programmer. His aim was to make a major leap forward in the world of word processing. But he soon discovered that something different was required. These early computers were just too slow using the existing programming languages. So he created his own programming language and devised a cunning algorithm to achieve the speed necessary to make the first the world's WYSIWYG word processor. He coded the first drop-down menus, and a host of other features which today are taken for granted.

The world recovered from recession and he found himself being pressed by old contacts in the world of hospitals to use his design and innovative skills to produce stylish modern furniture for the private hospitals which were being built all over the country. And his short but productive foray into the world of software came to an end.

Approaching 60, he decided to retire. But after turning his workshops into business units he became bored. Not enough was happening to keep him busy and happy. He couldn't find a tenant for one of the units and so decided he would have a go at being a chef and starting a little restaurant. A restaurant with a difference. Which is where this story began. How do I know David? Everyday Leader, my company, has its office and training room in one of David's business units.

As leaders, we are constantly looking for what is working well and what could be even better, in order to improve our position. The skill of being able to innovate is key to that. The Oxford dictionary definition for innovate is 'make changes in something established, especially by introducing new methods, ideas, or products.'

Seth Godin, in his book Tribes, highlights how leaders need to 'be a unicorn in a balloon factory', willing to disrupt the status quo and to create new ways of thinking to make improvements. So, as a leader, what is the process of innovation? What framework does it need to sit within to make it purposeful? I think there are five key questions that help a leader innovate:

- What is the end goal that you have in mind?
- What does good practice look like?
- What is the problem, hurdle or hindrance?
- What thing needs to change to make it even better?
- What are the different ways of approaching it?

What is the end goal you have in mind?

"Hello Colin, good to see you again," said Simon, as he shook my hand. "I loved what you said about high performing teams at the Chamber of Commerce event yesterday."

I had met Simon the day before and I was about to learn from him, just as he had from me the day before. "So Simon, tell me about your business," I asked him. Simon Jones is Projects Director for ERF Electrical, an electrical parts business, supplying electrical hardware such as cabling and sockets to electricians. He wanted the best products at the lowest prices and a great service. I asked him how he made sure his business was successful and he told me about a recent innovation.

He realised that the best way to get business was to ensure that he met the greatest need that building contractors wanted. There was a very large building contract locally. It was worth a lot of money to him if he could guarantee they used him and not online suppliers. So, he asked them if they were happy with his service and what they really wanted from a supplier and what their ideal service would look like. They liked his service but they then described their ideal service. The building company realised that they had their electricians spending a lot of time processing the electrical delivery, checking, signing and taking the order in. They said that in an ideal world all of that would be done for them, leaving the trained electricians to continue installing electrics. So Simon came up with an idea. He paid for a container to be delivered to their site and installed locks so that the building contractor and his van driver had keys. He racked out the container and arranged that the van driver would load the delivery into the container and lock it up and then visit the site foreman to have the delivery signed off. This arrangement cost him the cost of a shipping container but ensured that they ordered from him as they offered a unique service. At the end of the contract he retained the container and could use it on other similar jobs. His end goal was to maintain a large contract.
He calculated the cost of the container was a small cost to pay in comparison to the profit to be made and so his innovation of a new kind of delivery service helped him achieve his end goal.

One of the craziest things I have done is buy a double-decker bus. It was for good reason though. I was headteacher of a school and although it was a large school, we were desperate for space.
We needed to find somewhere for small groups of children to do breakout work or interventions for individuals with a teaching assistant. Like many schools, though, we did not have the funds to build with bricks and mortar. So what could we do? We weighed up options. Modular building, converting internal spaces. All of them were too expensive. "Maybe we should buy a double-decker bus," said Nic, one of the teachers. And so we did. We checked with the council whether planning permission was needed and it was not, as it was a vehicle. So my business manager set about looking and we found one in Yorkshire that was already converted for learning.

Now, neither of us was a bus driver, so we found a parent at the school who was, and the bus was delivered. It needed some remodelling on the outside, but the inside was ideal for the small groups. Our goal was that we needed a space for small groups and the children loved this as a place to learn in. Now, for a little honesty and a little piece of advice for anyone planning something similar; check and double-check things. As it turned out, after a complaint from a neighbour, the planning office decided it did need planning permission after all for it to be a workspace, despite an earlier email confirming it didn't need it. So, knowing your end goal is important, but so too is knowing 100% that you have the legal bases covered.

What does good practice look like?

So, if we are going to 'make changes in something established, especially by introducing new methods, ideas, or products', we need to know what the established best practice is. Then we unpick what are the shortfalls that we can innovate to make even better.

Anna, Shaun and I were three local headteachers that had hit it off ever since we started in 3 local schools in Ipswich in 2007. So, within a few years we formed a group we named as Triad, to review best practice in each other's schools and nationally. In 2009, when Ofsted released a document entitled 'Twenty Outstanding Primary Schools – Excelling against the Odds', we had a good read to identify what these schools were doing compared to our schools. Our schools faced some social challenges and we found ourselves intrigued to see what good practice looked like in a school in a similar circumstance to ours. We found one that had the closest matched demographics and so we arranged a road trip – well, a flight actually, as the three of us headed up to North Tyneside to visit Shiremoor Primary School. Seeing first-hand what Ofsted deemed as good practice allowed us to see where we met this and what we needed to innovate differently to adapt to our context. Only by seeing good practice could we know what could be developed further. With Simon and his electrical parts business, he knew what good practice looked like, but by speaking to the customer he was able to innovate to build on this. Good practice becomes the foundation to build innovation upon. So, what is the best practice in your field? Have you been to visit it to see what they do well? Without it, your innovation will be built on wobbly foundations.

What does the customer need?

Have you ever unpicked why you buy things that people advertise? The basic principles of why people buy things are:
"What are you offering? Will it help me? What do I need to do to acquire it?" At the centre of all of this is that it is something that the person needs (or thinks they need). So, in the story earlier of Simon, the electrical wholesaler, he recognised that the building contractor needed to keep his electricians on the job, so designed a service that met their needs and was cost effective.

In the case of David Wicks and his 745 restaurant, he recognised that customers were looking for a different experience. He saw that customers wanted good quality food and wanted wine to accompany it at sensible prices. The dining experience was different, more like treating you guests as friends at a dinner party, than a restaurant. Keeping the menu to a set meal enabled the best quality ingredients at sensible prices and no wastage. Its reputation spread fast and there was a waiting list to attend. All of it because it was what the customer was looking for.

I have suffered a variety of poor training courses in my teaching and leadership career. So when I started my leadership development company, I thought about what people wanted from a training course.

- It met need – training that addressed current issues of leadership.
- It had rich thinking in it. It needed to not only tell people what to do but the 'why' that sat behind it. In other words, to share research and ideas of the psychology of leadership with people.
- It was enjoyable. Enjoyment embeds learning.
- PowerPoints were clear and not full of text. Simple pictures and diagrams are far easier to remember than a page full of text.
- There were activities that embedded thinking and learning and were fun. Gutters and balls, counters, coloured mats. All were used as metaphors to help embed understanding.

Now, in one sense this is not ground-breaking, but compared to many training courses in the area, it has simple innovation. Diagrammatic PowerPoints, leadership psychology and metaphor games. This resulted in high feedback scores and comments from participants that it was really helpful.

I also thought about what would be useful to the organisation sending the participants. From working with schools, I knew that they had to justify the impact of training and that it was value for money. So, if I was running training for a school or cluster of schools, I collected the feedback scores and comments from participants and sent a summary to the host organisation. This could then be used to give to governors, trustees, or the board to show immediate impact.

What is the problem or hindrance?

In the late 1970s, James Dyson became fed up with his vacuum cleaner's diminishing performance as the bag became full. As he was already an inventor, he set about making a better version and after 5,127 prototypes he launched the 'G-Force' cleaner in 1983. Initially the UK manufacturing market rejected it, as it would disrupt the £100 million market for disposable cleaner bags. So, he launched it in Japan, winning a design award in 1991 and then set up his own manufacturing company. Like Seth Godin's unicorn in a balloon factory he disturbed the market, all driven by a response to solve a problem – that of diminishing suction power.

Now, when it comes to a vacuum cleaner, the problem and reason for it was obvious enough for James Dyson to find. In my experience as a coach, sometimes the problem that needs solving is not the first obvious one. For example, people will come to a coach wanting help to change the behaviour of someone on their team.
The problem here is that you can't change someone else's behaviour; only they can change that. Where it starts is how you manage your own behaviour and how you respond to them, and then you may be able to influence their behaviour.

So, the key here is not to jump to the obvious problem but to try to get to the root of the issue. Take time to ask yourself questions that probe deeper. A basic trick is the *Why, What, How* technique. It is important to clearly understand what sits at the root of why something is happening. You ask "Why?" and come up with an answer. Then you ask why *that* is happening. Keep asking yourself why, I suggest up to five times, until the true underlying cause is reached. Once you are clear on the reason why it is happening you can consider what might improve this. Lastly you ask how you could do something differently.

Why?	Ask yourself "Why?" 5 times.
What?	Ask yourself what might help eliminate this.
How?	Think about how you could innovate or do something differently.

Take an issue like a member of the team whose behaviour is causing the team difficulties. Let's call her Ethel. In this case, Ethel is not completing her tasks following meetings. So, the question is: *Why is Ethel not completing her tasks on time?*

Questions	Possible reasons			
Why? Possible reasons	1. She is not clear on the tasks	2. She does not have the skills to complete it		3. She has got too much work on - are we asking her to do too much?
Why?	Our minutes are not clear enough	Our recruitment for posts is not rigorous enough	We don't have a training programme	We don't have enough staff in this department

Why?	We don't have a minute taker in meetings	We don't have clear job descriptions	We don't have staff on the team who can develop this or a learning platform	Because it is a new department that is a new venture
Why?	We have not asked anyone to attend or take minutes	No-one is dedicated to write them	Because they don't have those skills	There has not been a review of the new department and its position
Why?	We just got into a bad habit	We don't have an HR department	Because that is not our field of business	There was not a review date set when it was set up
What might help?	Ask for someone to minute	Purchase HR advice	Work with another training company to develop a blended learning programme linked to national accreditation	Review of work teams to meet demand
	Recap at the end of the meeting so people are clear on their task and dates	Clearer job descriptions for recruitment		
	Clearer minutes			
How might we innovate?	The minute secretary completes work tracking software in the meeting	Online job packs for each job type for applicants and HR	Blended learning online and with training sessions	6-month review for all teams on what is working well and what could be better

What needs to change?

Appreciative thinking is a key mindset as a leader. Appreciative thinking starts from a position of 'positive first', considering what is working well. It then considers areas for development: what needs to be even better.

This allows you to build from a position of strength and tweak what is needed, rather than change things that are already working well. Innovation is built on the need to change: something can be done even better. You will see in the case of Ethel, above, that we considered what would help and how we might do things differently and be innovative.

What are the different ways of approaching it?

So, now you know that something needs to change and to be done differently, how do you generate an innovative approach it? I think it is about 'C'ing it differently.

Curious	Ask questions. What do I know works? What is not working? Why do I think it isn't? What human factors might affect this? What system factors might affect it? What is the culture? Is that helping or hindering?
Challenge	Challenge even the strongest held principles. For example, Dyson challenged the concept of having a bag in a vacuum cleaner.
Creative	Reimagine what it could look line. So, my 1985 slide projector had the light moving rather than the slides moving.
Collaborate	What are others doing in a different field? Are there like-minded groups I could partner with?

Consider Experiment, test things out. Be prepared to fail, but understand failure is not the end, just one way not to do it. Learn through failure.

When we had an issue with boys' writing, we applied this approach:

Curious Does writing have to be in books? Does it have to be with pencils or pens?

Challenge Do we have to be at desks?

Collaborate We formed a team of like-minded staff who wanted to try new ways of thinking. We said they could experiment and if it went wrong that was ok. No judgements on their teaching whilst this was going on.

Creative Liz, one of my innovative teachers, set up some experiments. She took away books and got the boys to work with big pens and sugar paper.

Consider The group tested their ideas. They came back and talked openly about what was working and what was not. It was ok to say, "Actually, this didn't work brilliantly."

Driver for all innovation

Whether you are starting a new restaurant, solving a problem in school or trying to win more business, innovation is a tool to solve it. Key to it all is, again, "What is the purpose and why do I want to do it?" Like a bamboo stick next to the growing plant, this acts as the guide to innovation.

Innovate
1 What is the end goal you have in mind?
2 What does good progress look like?
3 What thing needs to change to make it even better?
4 What is the problem, hurdle or hinderance?
5 What are the different ways of approaching it?
• NEW IDEAS • NEW METHODS • NEW PRODUCTS
7.45 PM
AIM
WHY?
WHY?
WHAT?
HOW?
curious
challenge
creative
collaboration
consider
©Everyday People/ ©Jane Ryder

Personal Reflection – Innovate

Unicorn in a Balloon Factory
Consider your field. What things really need shaking up and disrupting?
What would you like it to look like? What is your end goal?

Personal Reflection – Innovate

Innovation Components

How innovative are you? Which aspects could you develop? Score yourself 1-10 in these areas.

- 1-3 (I don't use much. I'm not confident in);
- 4-6 (I use and I am growing in confidence)
- 7-10 (I use and I am confident)

Consider one thing you could do to develop this.

Innovation	Score	One thing
End goal in mind		
Good practice		
Considering what needs to change		
Analysing the root of the problem		
Ways of approach		

Innovation

Who do you have in your contact list that is innovative? Who will help you look at your field in a new way?

Chapter 12: Define Success

Colin

"I can reflect positively on my leadership, because although the question of what is success is a hard one, it is a question that I know my answer to. I have seen success as a leader. I have also seen challenges and failures. Do I deserve to be on the stage amongst all the other leaders? Most certainly yes. Would I win the competition? No. I still have work to do. Masterpieces were not painted in a day!"

What is success?

As a reader, you may be asking yourself, "Well, Colin has written a book, and led schools, charities and a business, so has he been successful? If people develop the skills in this book, will they be successful leaders?"

On the surface of it, the question seems really easy. Surely, it's a yes or no answer. But there is a bigger question that needs to be answered first . . . What is success? As a leader, as you stop, turn, look back at what you have accomplished, have you been successful? What truly is success?

There is a family mantra that my Granny would say to me, that I have in turn passed on to my children: *"Just remember, you can only do your best."* Granny, like many Grannies, had learnt wisdom in life. It is certainly true that rather than being hard on yourself for not achieving something, it is important that in any one moment you can only do the best with all the resources and skills you have, and providing that you know you gave of your best at that moment, that is all that you can do. But is that the meaning of success, just knowing that you have given of your best?

The dictionary will tell you that success is the 'accomplishment of an aim or purpose' or the 'good outcome of an undertaking'. The popular world view is that success is achieving wealth and status. As a leader, is that all being successful is all about? Is it really just about accomplishing aims or tasks successfully, achieving wealth and status? Or is there some deeper definition that we need to understand in order to measure leadership?

Who's got talent?

To help us to understand this, imagine a new type of talent show. Instead of musical prowess, acrobatics or magic tricks, this time each contestant steps forward before the judges and presents their leadership achievements.

Person number one steps forward. Smartly dressed in the latest suit, he reveals how he has built a company from scratch. 5 years later he has sold it for several million pounds. He has retired at 45 and is enjoying a carefree lifestyle.

Number two is then ushered on. She's an executive leader. She has run several companies. She has a reputation for turning around failing companies, metaphorically grabbing them by the scruff of the neck and sorting them out. Financial results have gone up in her time. She takes no prisoners and believes in a tough approach. Very few original staff are left by the end of each of her tenures but that is ok in her mind as the job is done and she can move on to the next company. She expects her name to appear in the New Year's honours list soon.

Number three is an executive headteacher. She runs three schools. She looks baggy eyed and exhausted but her schools perform well. She is rigorous in her follow up and only employs the best teachers. Anyone who doesn't perform is encouraged on their way. She doesn't really like being as snappy and irritable as she is with her staff but they need to know results are the priority and her schools must be in the top band nationally. She can't let her reputation as a National Leader in Education be tarnished.

Number four is a CEO of a charitable trust that helps young people with drug and alcohol issues. She has paid staff and volunteers and she expects a lot of them. 80 hours a week is nothing to her. It's what needs to be done for the young people that the charity serves. She expects the same high standards and commitment of her staff and volunteers. She has improved the image of the charity considerably and it is gaining national recognition. The data shows that the work they do is helping young people.

Number five steps confidently onto stage. He is sharply dressed, clothing from a well-known tailor in London. He has learnt over time who to make connections with and as a result he has managed to rise through the ranks to lead a significant player in the food industry. He oversees sites across the United Kingdom. His theory of leadership is simple. Gather hard working individuals beneath him and let them do the work. He focuses on the networking with the big players and the contracts just seem to come in.

Number six, head slightly bowed, walks quietly on stage. She looks at the crowd, expecting the usual chorus of 'Imposter, imposter' that she hears in her mind, but the crowd sit there awaiting the announcement. From humble beginnings in a low-income single parent family, and facing challenging personal circumstances and health problems, she has worked her way up from the bottom. She was determined to do well, studying for her degree with the Open University alongside her day job. Shop floor worker, supervisor and now she is a department head. Results in her department are always the best, as she makes sure she gives each of her team the personal attention they need to help develop them. One day she hopes to set up her own business, but for now, her role is to be the best she can be and help others to be the same.

And then amongst these fictional characters, who bear resemblance to leaders we meet in our workplace, step onto stage the everyday leaders you have read about already. Matt who at 22 has built on his determination to redo his A levels, working conscientiously and gaining two promotions in his new job. Jenny, building on her teacher qualification to be a year leader. Simon, using his experience as a headteacher and pastoral skills to help children, parents and staff with Special Educational Needs. Lauren, who has taken her experience as a deputy head to now establish an education advisory company working with hundreds of school leaders and staff to develop education. Anna, CEO of an academy trust, helping turn around other schools joining the trust. Julian, Susan, Dave, Liz, Cyril. One by one they walk on stage. And lastly, you, the reader. It's your turn to join them.

Each leader on stage demonstrates an element of leadership and has had success. The judges turn and collaborate. The audience collaborate too, each with their own view.

If you were a judge or in the audience, who would you choose? Who would you put through to the next round or make your winner? What is successful leadership? What is accomplishment? What is achievement? What criteria would you use to judge them?

Reframing Success Criteria

The typical world view gravitates towards leadership that is tough, no nonsense and gets either financial, reputational, goal-orientated or academic achievement. There is an African word, Ubuntu, which means 'I am human because of the other'. This reflects that humanity has care of others at its core.

Good leaders lift people up and success in leadership reflects Ubuntu. I would propose that true success and accomplishment has a deeper moral, even spiritual, dimension that reflects this.

Successful leadership is when...

- the positive impact on people's lives lasts longer than the leader's physical presence.

- people see qualities, skills and behaviour in the leader that they then copy and model themselves.
- the leader is talked about for their actions of compassion and integrity in challenging circumstances.
- this has been achieved without breaking the leader themselves. It is successful because the leader knows the importance of balance in their life.

Successful leadership does get results, but it is there for the long haul, seeing the development of people as part of the journey and critical for success. Academic or financial success is interwoven with people development and not at the expense of people.

A successful leader is one who 'Knows, Shows and Grows'.

Knows Knows themselves well – strengths & weaknesses.
Knows balance (how to balance their life).
Knows their passion (what energises them).
Knows their goal and purpose.

Shows Shows their skills in their area of passion.
Shows others how to do the job well – enables them.

Grows Grows & develops others.
Grows & develops high performing teams.
Grows the organisation and its capacity for further growth.
Gets results in its field: financial, academic (schools), output goals or needs met (charities).
Grows themselves through self-reflection.
Grows the reputation of the organisation.

Now, if these were the criteria that you judge success by then we maybe have a winner or winners.

How do you judge yourself?

My son loves football and is a walking encyclopaedia of facts. Occasionally, he will ask me who is the greatest player or which is the best goal. Healthy debate then ensues. How do we decide? Well, we never start by deciding on the criteria and to be honest there is normally some bias on both sides that may sway us. To be objective we need to consider criteria. Does the best goal have to have teamwork, bravery, skill, shooting from distance? What makes a great goal? If I think it is teamwork and skill, but my son thinks it is dribbling and shooting long distance then we will have different views on various goals. As we consider whether we have been successful leaders, it is important to consider the criteria.

In my role as a leadership coach, one thing that I come across is this key statement that I use in training, and is a key part of the Emerging Leaders Leadership for Life training: *Our performance equals our potential minus interference.* Or, written as an equation:

Performance = Potential – Interference

Interference is anything that hinders our thinking and performance. Sometimes that can be that we think we are not good enough or that the situation is hopeless. If as a leader, we don't evaluate our success correctly, it will become an interference to us.
If we just see success as data performance or financial success, then anything short of that will be seen as a failure. It then becomes a nagging voice of interference. However, if we use the full width of leadership success criteria, that I considered earlier, then it allows us to have a more balanced review of our success and can pinpoint areas for us to develop.

There is a grid that I use to help people understand their feelings and the feelings of others when considering situations.

	Competence	Incompetence
Conscious		
Unconscious		

When we are conscious of our competence, we know we are performing well and feel good about ourselves. It can be a happy place to be.

When we are unconscious of our incompetence, when we don't know we are performing poorly, we are quite happy. We may be deluded about our performance but still happy because of that.

Equally there are two places that can be unhappy places to be in.

When we are unconscious of our competence, when we don't know we are good, we can feel sad. Equally when we are conscious of our incompetence, when we know we have performed poorly, it again causes sadness.

In the context of judging our success, if we don't use the right criteria we could be misinforming ourselves. For example if the money or data is strong we may think we are in the conscious competence of being a great leader. However, if we are having little or no positive impact on people's lives or development then may actually be in the other box of unconscious of our failings.

If our numbers, financial or data is a little down and we judge it just by that we may see ourselves as failing, and therefore in an unhappy place. Failure to see the wider impact of our leadership as success means we remain in the unconscious competence box. We are unaware of our wider success.

Masterpieces weren't painted in a day

I was asked the question, by my friend Lauren, "Have you been successful as a leader?" It is a challenging question and to be honest it would be best to ask my former staff and community I worked with. My belief is that if you are successful as a leader, you don't need to big yourself up and tell everyone how successful you are, because others will do it for you. As I consider this question of myself, I reflect on a range of things.

Did any of my schools win awards from the Department for Education or Ofsted? Did they appear in educational journals for their ground-breaking approach? No they did not.

Did I turn them around from a lower starting position? Those who worked there or attended would say yes, although my final Ofsted inspection did not reap the recognition the school deserved.

But success as a leader is not just judged by academic or financial performance. Clearly the leader needs to make a difference in the area their organisation works in, but this alone is not pure success.
As a leader, I have been able to work through the skills listed in the chapters of this book. I have gained a wisdom of what is important and how to manage failure. I have inspired people to lead, to step out and take new challenges. I have developed them in their roles and developed them into leaders. Indeed, my proudest element in leadership is that 14 of my former staff became headteachers themselves. I have led with integrity and during times of challenge. Problem-solving has often been tackled on a daily basis whilst leading staff strategically.

I can reflect positively on my leadership, because although the question of what is success is a hard one, it is a question that I know my answer to. I have seen success as a leader. I have also seen challenges and failures. Do I deserve to be on the stage amongst all the other leaders? Most certainly yes. Would I win the competition? No. I still have work to do. Masterpieces were not painted in a day!

'With great power comes great responsibility'
2
People copy the leader's skills
3
Compassion
Integrity
SUPPORT
CHALLENGE
QUESTION
Performance = Potential – Interference
COACH
Whatever you do, do your best
Have honest and open review- it will help you grow
Good leaders lift others up
4
The leader doesn't break themselves
How can I help you get there?
You have amazing potential
SUCCESS
Transforms lives
5
Development of others
Go try it out
1
Positive impact
Just remember you can only do your best
A successful leader:
Knows
Shows
Grows
'I've learned that people will forget what you said, people will forget what you did, but people will never forget how you made them feel.'
Maya Angelou
Define Success

Epilogue

As a child, like many other children, I loved the Panini football sticker albums. I loved collecting and sticking the different footballers. Each year though, I never finished the album, but that did not matter; it was the starting, the collecting, the swapping, the taking part. It is a common error for people to look at those who have been in leadership for many years and to think, "I can never be like that." To compare yourself to them and give up before you have even started. In truth, every leader has started from somewhere and the key is to start. Like the sticker album, gather the skills that you have at the moment and then keep taking part and collect the skills as you go along. If it will help, there is an Everyday Leader Skills Wheel at the end of this book. Consider where you are on each segment, based on what you have read in the chapter, scoring yourself out of ten on your current position, and set yourself a target on where you would like to be in each section. You can find and print a copy of the wheel overleaf or at: www.everydayleader.co.uk/everydaybookresources .

My grandparents and parents instilled a mantra in me as a child – "We don't mind what you do as long as you do your best." Now I am sure they would have been disappointed if I had become a bank robber and did my best at it, but I understood what they meant. If I was to give you some mantras for leadership it would be the following:

- **You have amazing potential . . .** go try it out.
- **Whatever you do, do your best.** Try your best at whatever you lend your hand to . . . but don't get swallowed in disappointment if it doesn't quite go to plan.
- **Have open and honest review** – it will help you grow. When things don't go well . . . learn for the next occasion.

- **Good leaders lift others up.** Do it all with humility and love and care of those you are leading.

"With great power comes great responsibility." Now, whether you attribute this to Voltaire or Peter Parker's Uncle Ben in Spiderman, the phrase certainly applies to leadership. Good leaders lift people up to better things. Bad leaders push people down so that they appear stronger themselves. It is an honour and a privilege to lead people and it must always be done in the spirit of integrity, honesty and care for your followers.

When we lead, we must remember the words of Maya Angelou: *"'I've learned that people will forget what you said, people will forget what you did, but people will never forget how you made them feel."*

It is crucial, when following my four mantras above or when using the skills of this book, that you lead with integrity, creating experiences where those that follow you will remember you for how you made them feel empowered and lifted them up to better things, even in the most challenging situations.

Leadership is not for the elite. Leadership is for everyday people. So go and be an everyday leader and lead yourself and those around you, in whatever situation you find yourself. Lead well.

Everyday Leader

www.everydayleader.co.uk

Leadership Skills Wheel

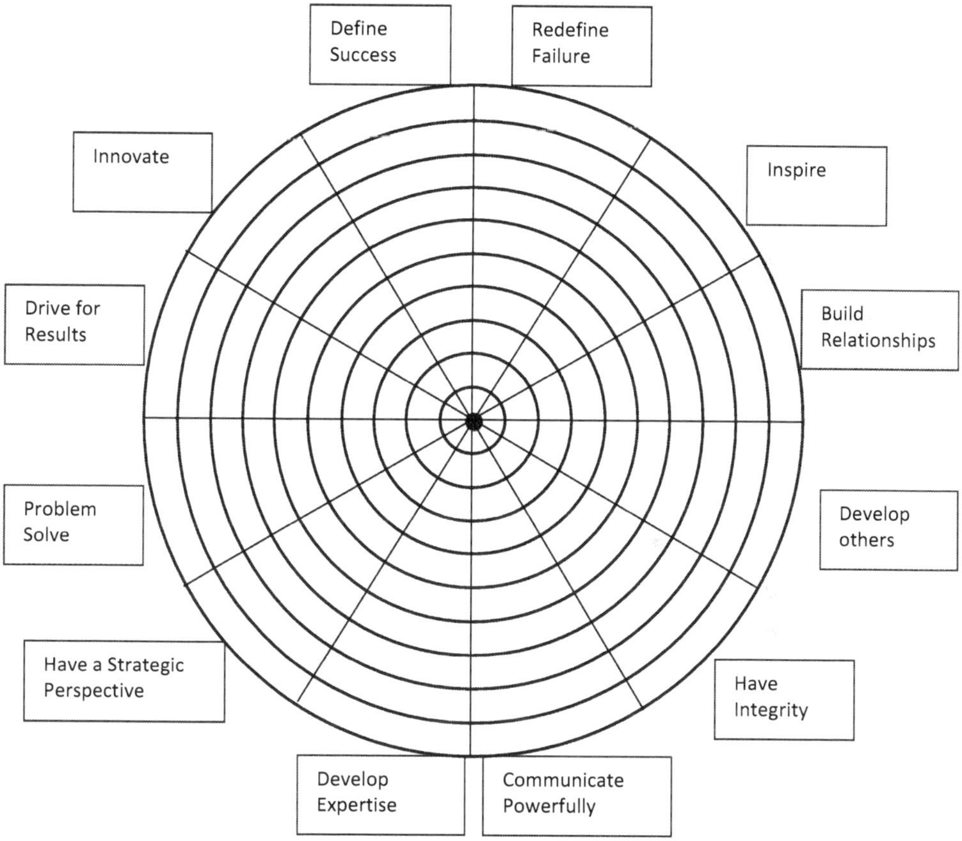

The leadership wheel doesn't have to be complicated.

1. Give yourself a gut feel score out of 10 for each section.
2. Colour it in from the centre outwards to reflect the score.
3. Look at the wheel. Which area is your strongest? Which area could be developed?
4. Read the chapter again that needs to be developed. What 3 things could you try to develop your skills in this area?

Artistry

Character illustrations and infographics created by Jane Ryder

Credits

If you've not grasped it already, I wanted this book to be one that would help everyday people realise that everyday leadership is accessible. I'm indebted to people who have helped me discover that and so, please forgive me – it is my first book after all – if I pay a little thanks to them.

Everyday people who have displayed extraordinary leadership have appeared as characters in this book. I'm thankful for their agreement to appear, but most of all thankful for having met them and learnt from them. Whether it is my youth leader like Cyril Wearn or a colleague like Jenny Gooch, I have learnt a lot from you. I have learnt everyday leadership skills, and I hope the book has now helped others to learn from them too.

Faithful friends are always important in life, even more so when you take a plunge to take a new direction and write a book. Steve & Margaret Jackman, Tracy & Julian Eddy, Dave & Miranda Courteen, Ian & Lorna Macauley, Kim & Dave Burgess, Steve & Clare Miles, Trevor Waldock & Jane Beaumont, Lauren Meadows & Dave Lightowler. Your support has fuelled the fire when needed most, especially over the last three years.

Fellow leaders, Dave, Anna, Shaun, Simon, Lee, Sue, Gill, Kelly & Tracy who stood by me and endorsed me, as I started my leadership development business. Your support helped me be braver.

The practical feedback and proof reading from Catherine Legg and Lauren Meadows has been crucial to ensure the grammar police are kept at bay and so readers can make sense of the book. Your precision is crucial. Thank you for your patience and grace.

My thanks to Jane Ryder for her book illustrations and infographics. Her creativity is wonderful. Thank you for your patience with me.

But there are some people whose investment in me and my leadership has been deep and rich.

Firstly, thank you to my mum and dad. Their love and acceptance made it ok to make mistakes and their simple reminder of the importance of morality and integrity ensured that this has been the foundation of my leadership.

Secondly, to my grandparents. Granny was always interested in what I was doing, always valuing me as a person. Grandad modelled even more than the problem-solving techniques as Norman Savory of chapter 8. Moral character, aspiration, hard work, care of others and perhaps most importantly a belief in his grandson. As he reached old age, he continued to instil value in me with his smile, with eyes lighting up when he saw I had come to visit. My hope is that my leadership reflects their value of others too.

My parents started the work and my beautiful wife, Lisa, continues to help shape me. She has smoothed off my rough edges, infusing some of her patience, compassion and thoughtfulness in me in the process. Her beauty goes beyond her looks and anyone who spends time with Lisa sees the beauty of her caring nature and compassion. Her support of me in life and in leadership has been unwavering. Thank you for your confidence in me, which helps me, in turn, to bring that to others.

And finally, to my children, Sophie, Matt and Emily. Like all families, there are times when Dad annoys kids and kids annoy Dad. But, thankfully, these are not often in our household. I am incredibly proud of the adults you have become. Thank you for your patience when I have been shut away working on the book or developing the new leadership company. Thank you for your public support of me as a dad and as a leader. My hope and prayer is that you will all go on to exceed what I have achieved, not only as an everyday person, but as an everyday leader.

Videos

Would you like to know more about the leaders in this book? We have a collection of videos where leaders in the chapters are interviewed. Visit the site to watch the videos.

Video Resource on
www.everydayleader.co.uk/everydaypeoplevideos

Chapter 1	Jenny Gooch & Matt Tapscott
Chapter 2	Dave Hannah
Chapter 3	Liz Green
Chapter 4	Paul Wilcox
Chapter 5	Simon Phillips
Chapter 6	Dave Courteen
Chapter 7	Lauren Meadows
Chapter 8	Julian Eddy
Chapter 9	Trevor Waldock
Chapter 10	Anna Hennell James
Chapter 11	David Wicks

Resources

Resources mentioned in the book can be found at
www.everydayleader.co.uk/everydaybookresources

Endnotes

---

[i] Howard Gardner – *Leading Minds: An Anatomy of Leadership*. (New York: Basic Books, 1995). ISBN-13: 978-0465027736

[ii] Seth Godin – *Tribes: We need you to lead us.* Piatkus Books (6 Nov. 2008) ISBN-13: 978-0749939755

[iii] Matthew Syed – *Black Box Thinking.* John Murray; 01 edition (7 April 2016) ISBN-13: 978-1473613805

[iv] Leadership For life is a programme to help the poorest communities lead themselves to overcome the challenges that they face. The material is based on timeless leadership principles. www.emergingleaders.co.uk

[v] Howard Gardner – *Leading Minds: An Anatomy of Leadership*. (New York: Basic Books, 1995). ISBN-13: 978-0465027736

[vi] Seth Godin – *Tribes: We need you to lead us.* Piatkus Books (6 Nov. 2008) ISBN-13: 978-0749939755

[vii] Daniel Goleman, Richard E. Boyatzis, Annie McKee – *Primal Leadership. Unleashing the Power of Emotional Intelligence.* Harvard Business Review Press; Anniversary edition (6 Aug. 2013) ISBN-13: 978-1422168035

[viii] Mary Myatt – *High Challenge Low Threat*. John Catt Educational Ltd (16 April 2016) ISBN-13: 978-1909717862

[ix] Matthew Syed – *Bounce.* Fourth Estate (GB) (1 April 2011) ISBN-13: 978-0007350544

[x] https://www.ncbi.nlm.nih.gov/pmc/articles/PMC2907136/

[xi] Emmons, R. A. & McCullough, M. E. (2003) *Counting blessings versus burdens: An experimental investigation of gratitude and subjective well-being in daily life,* Journal of Personality and Social Psychology 84: 377-89

[xii] Dehydroepiandrosterone (DHEA) and Dehydroepiandrosterone Sulfate (DHEA-S)

[xiii] Leadership For Life is a programme to help poor communities lead themselves to overcome the challenges that they face. The material is based on timeless leadership principles. www.emergingleaders.co.uk

[xiv] Seth Godin – *Tribes: We need you to lead us.*(Piatkus Books (6 Nov. 2008) ISBN-13: 978-0749939755

[xv] Steven Covey – *7 Habits of Highly Effective People.* Simon and Schuster; Reprinted Edition (4 Jan. 2004) ISBN-13: 978-0684858395

[xvi] Simon Sinek – *Start with Why.* Penguin; 01 edition (6 Oct. 2011) ISBN-13: 978-0241958223

[xvii] Jerome Bruner, *Actual Minds, Possible Worlds.* Harvard University Press; New edition (1 July 1986) ISBN-13: 978-0674003668

[xviii] Steve Adams, *The Centre Brain: 5 Prompts to Persuasive Power.* SPCK Publishing (20 July 2017) ISBN-13: 978-0281077908

[xix] Trevor Waldock – *To Plant a Walnut Tree: How to Create a Fruitful Legacy By Using Your Experience* Nicholas Brealey Publishing (12 May 2011) ISBN-13: 978-1857885651

[xx] Harvard Business review March/April 2000

[xxi] Chris McChesney – *4 Disciplines of Execution: Achieving Your Wildly Important Goals* Simon & Schuster UK; UK ed. edition (21 July 2015) ISBN-13: 978-0857205834

Printed in Great Britain
by Amazon

43829105R00136